OUR CHANGING CONSTITUTION

HOW AND WHY WE HAVE AMENDED IT

Isobel V. Morin

The Millbrook Press
Brookfield, Connecticut

Cover photographs courtesy of Thomas Morlock;
Library of Congress; National Archives.
Photographs courtesy of Corbis-Bettmann: pp. 8, 23, 32, 80,
98, 109, 130, 141; © Renato Rotolo, Gamma Liaison: p. 46;
Library of Congress: p. 59; © 1978 Martin A. Levick: p. 148.

Library of Congress Cataloging-in-Publication Data
Morin, Isobel V., 1928-
Our changing Constitution : how and why we
have amended it / Isobel V. Morin
p. cm.
Includes bibliographical references and index.
Summary: Explores the amendments that have been made
to the Constitution, as well as the proposed amendments
that were not passed, detailing the controversies and
Supreme Court cases that surrounded them.
ISBN 0-7613-0222-0 (lib. bdg.)
1. Constitutional amendments—United States—Juvenile
literature. [1. Constitutional amendments—United States.]
I. Title.
KF4557.M67   1998
342.73'03—dc21   97-26909   CIP   AC

Published by The Millbrook Press, Inc.
2 Old New Milford Road
Brookfield, Connecticut 06804

CONTENTS

OUR CHANGING CONSTITUTION

THE CONSTITUTIONAL CONVENTION

One late summer day in 1787 a small group of men gathered for the last time in the Pennsylvania State House, where the Declaration of Independence had been signed eleven years earlier, to view the document they had worked on for the past four months. The stifling summer heat, the incessant buzz of flies, and the noise of traffic filtering through the windows of the East Room had added to the difficulty of their job. Still, they persisted in the task they had set for themselves. And now the finished product lay before them on the table: Four sheets of parchment covered with fine script, beginning with the preamble, "WE THE PEOPLE of the United States . . . do ordain and establish this Constitution for the United States of America" and ending with the words, "Done in Convention by the Unanimous Consent of the States present the Seventeenth Day of September in the Year of Our Lord one thousand seven hundred and Eighty seven and of the Independence of the United States of America the Twelfth."

Even if they had enjoyed greater comfort, the men who gathered in Philadelphia that summer faced a daunting task. Officially their job was to revise the Articles of Confederation—the written agreement under which the union of thirteen former British colonies had

The framers of the Constitution knew that the
document they had produced was imperfect and would
face many challenges. Indeed, the very process of
writing and ratifying it was filled with controversy. This
drawing shows George Washington addressing the
Constitutional Convention in Philadelphia, in 1787.

operated for the past six years. However, some of the delegates to the 1787 convention wanted to go much further. They wanted to scrap the Articles altogether and write a new agreement that would create one nation out of thirteen independent and often quarrelsome states. They believed that the union's survival required the establishment of a government strong enough to override the conflicting interests of the individual states and to stand up to the European powers that might easily overwhelm them. The new government couldn't be too strong, however, because the states might not agree to anything that took away too many of their powers.

THE ARTICLES OF CONFEDERATION

The weakness of the Articles had been apparent for some time. This agreement, in effect since March 1781, provided for neither an executive officer to carry out the laws that the Confederation Congress passed nor judges to rule on questions concerning these laws. Congress had the authority to appoint and direct officers of the army and navy, to make decisions regarding peace and war, to handle affairs with foreign countries and Indian tribes, to set the value of coins, and to establish post offices. It had little real power, however. It could tax neither the states nor the people. Congress also lacked the power to regulate commerce among the states or with foreign countries. In addition, major laws required the approval of all thirteen states. This last requirement removed any chance for correcting defects in the Articles, since one state, Rhode Island, consistently refused to approve amendments.

In the absence of a strong central government, the individual states took matters into their own hands. They taxed imports from other states, issued their own paper money (which often quickly became worthless), and quarreled over boundaries. Although the states were often at odds with one another, they sometimes did cooperate in resolving mutual problems. For example, in March 1785, Maryland and Virginia reached an agreement on navigation rights on the Potomac River, the waters of which were shared by the two states. Encouraged by the success of this undertaking, Virginia called for an interstate convention the following year to explore the possibility of establishing a uniform system of commercial regulation among the states.

The meeting took place in September 1786 in Annapolis, Maryland. But only twelve delegates from five states (Delaware, New Jersey, New York, Pennsylvania, and Virginia) attended it. With such a small attendance, the delegates couldn't accomplish much. They were committed to the idea, however. Before the meeting ended, they approved a report written by Alexander Hamilton of New York urging another meeting in Philadelphia the following May to consider whatever changes were needed to respond to the urgent needs of the union. There was no guarantee that Congress would agree to such a meeting or that the states would send delegates. After all, few were willing to give up power without a fight, even to deal with a national crisis, and not everyone agreed that a crisis existed.

SHAYS'S REBELLION

Events in Massachusetts soon convinced many Americans that a crisis did exist. In September 1786 a group of farmers in the western part of the state, under the leadership of Daniel Shays (a former army captain during the Revolutionary War), staged an armed rebellion against the state government. The farmers were angry because their land and other assets were being seized by the state because they were unable to pay their taxes, and some were even being imprisoned for failure to pay their debts. The state asked Congress for help in putting down the rebellion, but Congress couldn't provide an army big and strong enough to help. The state eventually persuaded its wealthiest citizens to provide money to hire troops, and in February 1787 the rebellion ended with the capture or flight of the rebel leaders, who were later pardoned.

The news of Shays's Rebellion alarmed many citizens of other states. If this could happen in Massachusetts, what could stop it from happening elsewhere? And how could the feeble central government restore order without money or troops? Before long, every state except Rhode Island appointed delegates to attend the proposed meeting in Philadelphia. On February 21, 1787, Congress, recognizing that the meeting was going to take place regardless of what it did, approved the gathering. However, wary of what the delegates might do, Congress stated that the meeting was for the sole and express purpose of revising the Articles of Confederation.

The group that met in Philadelphia wasn't very large. Seventy-four delegates were appointed, but only fifty-five actually went to Philadelphia to attend the meeting. (Rhode Island, continuing its pattern of refusal to cooperate with the other states, never sent any delegates.) Moreover, the average daily attendance at the convention was never more than about thirty delegates. However, this number included about twenty of the most dedicated advocates of a strong national government. Among them were George Washington, the Revolutionary War leader who had been coaxed out of retirement at his Virginia plantation; Washington's fellow Virginian James Madison (often called the Father of the Constitution); and the widely respected scholar age and various ailments that he had to be carried to the meetings. Notably, neither Thomas Jefferson nor John Adams were among the delegates present. Both were abroad at the time. The delegates also included signers of the Declaration of Independence, men who had fought in the Revolutionary War, current members of the Confederation Congress, and current or former members of state and local governments. This distinguished group lent legitimacy to the convention's undertaking—something that was essential to its success.

TWO MAJOR PLANS
FOR A NEW GOVERNMENT

Much of the debate during the convention centered around two proposed plans for establishing a new national government—the Virginia Plan and the New Jersey Plan. Governor Edmund Randolph of Virginia introduced the Virginia Plan on May 29, 1787. A few days later, Governor William Paterson of New Jersey introduced the New Jersey Plan as an alternative to Randolph's proposal.

The Virginia Plan

The Virginia Plan was designed to correct the most serious weaknesses of the Articles of Confederation. It called for a national government with three branches—legislative, executive, and judicial—instead of the single legislative body established by the Articles. There would be a single executive chosen by the legislative body, which would also choose the judges for the judicial branch. The legislative branch, which would have much broader powers than the Confederation Congress, would consist of two houses. Representation in each house would be determined according to either a state's population or the amount of money it contributed to-population or the amount of money it contributed toward the support of the central government.

The New Jersey Plan

The New Jersey Plan, the alternative, called for the continuation of a legislative body with a single house in which each state would have an equal vote. This plan called for an executive council instead of the single executive officer proposed under the Virginia Plan. The national legislature would also have fewer powers than those proposed under the Virginia Plan.

A DISPUTE OVER REPRESENTATION IN CONGRESS

The issue of representation in the proposed new Congress proved to be a thorny one. The delegates from states with small populations, fearful that they would be outvoted by the larger states, favored the New Jersey Plan. The delegates from the more heavily populated states understandably favored the Virginia Plan. After long and sometimes heated arguments on the two plans, neither side appeared willing to give in.

On July 2, matters came to a head. That day the convention voted on whether the states would have equal representation in the Senate, the upper house of the proposed new Congress. (The group had already decided that Congress would have two houses.) The result was a deadlock. At that point it looked as if the whole undertaking would collapse.

The Great Compromise

Then one of the South Carolina delegates offered a suggestion. Why not let a committee consisting of one member from each of the states try to work out a compromise? The convention quickly agreed, and the committee began two days of nonstop work, without even a pause to celebrate Independence Day. On July 5, it presented its proposal to the other delegates.

The committee's proposed compromise (often called the Great Compromise) didn't differ greatly from an earlier compromise the group had voted down. The Great Compromise called for representation in the lower house of Congress, the House of Representatives, based on population and filled by popular vote. In the upper house, the Senate, each state would have two members elected by its legislature. The committee sweetened the bargain for the larger states by requiring that all money-raising bills originate in the lower house. The larger states, because of their larger population, could be expected to bear the lion's share of any taxes Congress might impose. By requiring spending bills to originate in the House of Representatives, the committee gave these states greater control over taxes. The convention accepted the Great Compromise on July 16, 1787.

Another major controversy threatened to undo the convention's work: the issue of slavery. The controversy involved two main questions: First, should the central government have the power to regulate or forbid the further importation of slaves? Second, should slaves be counted in determining both the representation in the lower house of Congress and in the levying of taxes?

The convention settled the question regarding the importation of additional slaves by forbidding Congress from banning slave importation until 1808. (The delegates assumed—correctly, as it turned out—that Congress would impose such a ban as soon as it was authorized to do so.)

The delegates compromised on the counting of slaves for purposes of representation and taxation by providing that for these purposes all "free persons" and three-fifths of "all other persons" (meaning slaves) would be counted. This agreement is known as the Three-Fifths Compromise.

THE CONVENTION WORKS OUT THE DETAILS

Gradually the Constitution took shape. The powers of the three branches of the central government were described. The qualifications for federal officers, how they were to be chosen, the length of their terms of office, and provisions for removing them from office for misconduct were set down. Provisions for both ratification (or approval) and amendment of the Constitution were included.

Rules for Ratification

Mindful of Rhode Island's persistent refusal to go along with the wishes of the majority of the states, the convention decided not to require the approval of all thirteen states to put the Constitution into effect. Instead, it settled on nine, the number of states necessary to approve major decisions of Congress under the Articles of Confederation. The supporters of the Constitution were also afraid that the state legislatures would not vote in favor of a document that limited their powers. They therefore specified that ratification would be handled by conventions of the states' eligible voters.

We the People of the United States

After all of the main issues had been settled, a five-man committee drafted the final version of the proposed Constitution. This group made one important change in the wording of the preamble. It replaced the phrase 'We the people of the states of" with the words "We that the people themselves, not the states, were the real framers of the Constitution.

Lack of a Bill of Rights

When the finished document was presented to the assembly, a last-minute debate occurred on the question of whether it should include a bill of rights—a set of specific guarantees of the people's individual liberties. Two delegates—Elbridge Gerry of Massachusetts and George Mason of Virginia—proposed that a bill of rights be added to the Constitution. However, even though it had become clear that the people wanted a bill of rights, the convention turned down this proposal—a decision that could easily have resulted in the rejection of the Constitution.

THE SIGNING OF THE CONSTITUTION

The forty-one delegates who met for the last time on September 17, 1787, knew that the Constitution wasn't perfect. No document produced by a group with so many conflicting interests could have achieved perfection. Benjamin Franklin urged the delegates to sign it anyway. Franklin, who was too feeble to address the group himself, had his fellow Pennsylvanian James Wilson read his remarks for him. Franklin also proposed that the Constitution contain the words "Done in convention by the unanimous consent of the states present." This allowed delegates to sign the Constitution on behalf of their respective states even though they did not agree personally with all of its provisions.

In an attempt to persuade the convention to slow its push for a new government, Mason and a fellow Virginian, Edmund Randolph, suggested that state conventions be called to propose amendments to the Constitution. A second constitutional convention would then decide on these amendments before the Constitution was submitted to the states for ratification. The other delegates, fearful that this proposal would undo all the work of the past four months, quickly rejected it. Afterward, despite Franklin's urgings, Mason, Randolph, and Elbridge Gerry of Massachusetts refused to sign the Constitution. Gerry and Mason still believed it should contain a bill of rights, and all three men were concerned that it gave the central government too much power.

At last the moment for signing had arrived. George Washington, who had been elected president of the convention, was the first to sign. Then the delegates signed their names under the names of their states. Alexander Hamilton was the sole signer from New York—the two other New York delegates had left the convention earlier because they disagreed with its decisions. Two delegates each from Connecticut, Georgia, Massachusetts, New Hampshire, and Virginia signed. Three each from Maryland and North Carolina signed, along with four each from New Jersey and South Carolina. Five signatures were placed on the document by Delaware's four delegates present for the signing. George Read signed both his own name and that of John Dickinson, who had left due to illness. (Before leaving, Dickinson authorized Read to sign the document for him.) The largest number of signers, eight, came from the host state, Pennsylvania. After these men had signed their names, William Jackson, the convention secretary, added his name to attest to the other signatures.

And now, after almost four months, the group's work was completed. Or was it? The Constitution still had to be accepted by the Confederation Congress (no easy task, since the new Constitution would put this Congress out of business). Also, nine states had to ratify it before it could take effect.

RATIFICATION
AND DEMANDS FOR
AMENDMENTS

After the Philadelphia convention adjourned, the supporters of the Constitution had a dual job on their hands. In addition to explaining and justifying its provisions, they had to fend off demands for amendments.

The Constitution provides for two methods of amendment. One method requires that amendments be based on a two-thirds vote of each house of Congress, followed by ratification by three-fourths of the states. The other method allows two-thirds of the states to call for a constitutional convention to consider amendments, which will become part of the Constitution after three-fourths of the states ratify them. The framers of the Constitution hoped that consideration of any proposed amendments would be put off until after its adoption. As things turned out, however, the Constitution's supporters achieved its adoption only by promising to agree to a series of amendments proposed by the states.

CONGRESS SUBMITS THE
CONSTITUTION TO THE STATES

On September 28, 1787, only eleven days after the signing of the Constitution, Congress unanimously agreed to submit the document to the states for ratification without taking a position for or against it. In support of what the Convention had decided, Congress also asked the legislatures of each state to let conventions of the states' eligible voters decide whether to approve the Constitution.

FEDERALISTS AND ANTI-FEDERALISTS

In deciding whether to ratify the Constitution, supporters and opponents within each state argued at length over its provisions, both in the conventions and in newspapers and other periodicals. The opponents of the Constitution argued that the new government, because of its broad powers, would eventually destroy the independence of the states. The supporters of the Constitution tried their best to reassure the public on that score. They argued that the new government would not be radically different from the one under which the country was then operating. It would still be a federal system of government—one in which the states retained their powers in certain aspects of government while the central government was given powers in other aspects. To bolster this argument the supporters of the Constitution called themselves Federalists. They called the opponents of the Constitution Anti-Federalists.

DEMANDS FOR A BILL OF RIGHTS

Demands for amendments came up in several of the state ratifying conventions. The proposed amendments generally called for reductions in the power of one or more of the three branches of the central government and the inclusion of a bill of rights. These two issues were related. Many Americans were reluctant to establish a powerful national government. They certainly did not want such a government without assurance that it could not trample on their individual rights. They still remembered the actions that the British had taken to suppress the colonies' struggle for independence and how tyrannical they felt these actions were. Having shaken off one oppressive government, they wanted to make sure they weren't simply replacing it with yet another.

The Federalists defended the decision not to include a bill of rights by insisting that the Constitution itself protected the people's rights. Moreover, a list of specific rights might imply that the government was granting rights that the people didn't already possess, and that any rights not listed were not granted. These arguments weren't very convincing, however. A large majority of Americans still wanted their rights spelled out, and protected, by the Constitution.

THE RATIFICATION OF THE CONSTITUTION

At first the Federalists had smooth sailing despite the demands for amendments. By the middle of January 1788, five states—Delaware, Pennsylvania, New Jersey, Georgia, and Connecticut– had ratified the Constitution. Favorable votes from only four more states were needed for it to take effect. These votes were hard to obtain, however. The Federalists ran into stiff opposition in Massachusetts, New York, and Virginia.

The Massachusetts ratifying convention had a number of Anti-Federalist delegates, including such Revolutionary War figures as Samuel Adams and John Hancock. Nevertheless, the Federalists managed to obtain that state's ratification by a narrow margin on February 8, 1788, by agreeing to submit a list of recommended amendments along with the ratification.

The ratifying conventions in Virginia, New York, and New Hampshire all met in June 1788. (The New Hampshire convention first met in February of that year, but the Federalists, sensing that a majority of the delegates opposed ratification, managed to have further sessions postponed until June.) By that time Maryland and South Carolina had ratified the Constitution. Only one more state's ratification was needed. This was accomplished on June 21, 1788, when New Hampshire ratified the Constitution after recommending a series of amendments similar to those already proposed in Massachusetts. However, because of their size and location, the favorable votes of New York and Virginia were needed to ensure the survival of the new government. These two states were among the wealthiest and most heavily populated. Virginia had also played a large part in the struggle for independence, and a Virginian, George Washington, was the man most Americans wanted for the first president of the new government. Moreover, if either New York or Virginia remained outside the Union, it would be geographically split, causing potential problems with interstate commerce, finance, and travel.

In Virginia the debate was vigorous and often bitter. Once again the Anti-Federalists demanded constitutional amendments. Patrick Henry, who had argued so forcefully for independence from British rule, gave a series of impassioned speeches denouncing the entire Constitution. Edmund Randolph (who had refused to sign the Constitution but now supported it) warned the group that, since eight states had already ratified the Constitution, Virginia's real choice was whether or not to remain in the Union. Moreover, James Madison and the other Federalist delegates tried to win over their opponents by agreeing to support proposals for constitutional amendments provided they were only recommendations, not conditions for ratification. Madison also promised to push for a bill of rights in the new Congress if he were elected to that body. On June 25, 1788, the Virginia convention voted to ratify the Constitution without insisting that it be amended first.

In New York the Anti-Federalists far outnumbered the Federalist delegates. However, while the New York convention was meeting, news came of ratification by New Hampshire and Virginia. At that point the Anti-Federalists decided that it would be unwise to reject the Constitution outright and put New York outside the Union. They therefore shifted their attention to the issue of amendments. After drawing up a long list of amendments, including a bill of rights, New York ratified the Constitution on July 26, 1788.

The last two of the original thirteen states ratified the Constitution within two years after its adoption. After voting in August 1788 not to ratify the Constitution until a second constitutional convention considered a number of amendments, North Carolina changed its mind and ratified the Constitution on November 21, 1789. Rhode Island ratified it on May 29, 1790, after Congress threatened to cut off all trade with that stubborn state. By that time the first group of constitutional amendments had been sent to the states for ratification, further persuading Rhode Island to comply.

THE FIRST CONSTITUTIONAL AMENDMENTS

When the First Congress met, James Madison, who was a member of the House of Representatives, fulfilled the promise he had made during his election campaign by proposing several constitutional amendments to protect people's individual rights. The House agreed to seventeen amendments. The Senate cut the list to fourteen. In September 1789 the House and Senate agreed on twelve amendments, which were then sent to the states for ratification.

The ratification of the Constitution was
celebrated in New York City in 1789, where
the ship Hamilton passed a reviewing stand that
included members of Congress. Ratification was
cause for celebration, but it came only with
the condition that the Constitution would be
amended—and it was, with the Bill of Rights.

By December 15, 1791, the states had ratified ten amendments (the Bill of Rights). They failed to ratify the other two because they thought Congress already had the constitutional authority to make the changes that the two amendments would accomplish. One of the amendments would have revised the method of determining the number of seats in the House of Representatives. The other would have prevented alterations in congressional pay scales from taking effect until after an election. (See Chapter 12 for further discussion of these proposed amendments.)

Once the Bill of Rights was adopted, most Americans were satisfied with the Constitution, and didn't believe further amendments were needed. In more than two hundred years following its adoption, only seventeen more amendments have been passed. These amendments were added for various reasons. The Civil War resulted in three of them. The changes caused by the country's rapid industrialization, the shift of population from rural to urban areas, the massive waves of immigration that took place after the Civil War, and demands for more democratic provisions on elections and voting rights triggered additional amendments. Four amendments (the Eleventh, the Fourteenth, the Sixteenth, and the Twenty-Sixth) overturned previous Supreme Court decisions.

THE SUPREME COURT AND THE CONSTITUTION

The history of our changing Constitution is so closely tied to the history of the Supreme Court that one cannot be understood apart from the other. The Constitution doesn't spell out the Supreme Court's authority to rule on the constitutionality of federal and state laws. We can infer it, however, from both Article III, which describes the powers of the federal judiciary branch, and the debates during the 1787 convention and the ratification period.

Both the Federalists and the Anti-Federalists recognized that the Supreme Court would have the authority to rule on the meaning of the Constitution. One Anti-Federalist, writing under the pen name Brutus, considered this authority to be a dangerous concentration of power. He pointed out that there would be no way to appeal a Supreme Court decision because Congress would have no authority to overrule it. He also feared that the federal judicial power would eventually result in the complete destruction of the powers of the states. Brutus believed that the federal courts would lean strongly toward interpretations of the Constitution that were favorable to the central government's authority, and that these interpretations would perhaps even extend this authority.

Alexander Hamilton, writing in essay No. 78 of *The Federalist* (a collection of pro-Constitution articles written largely by Hamilton and James Madison) answered Brutus by describing the federal judiciary as the least dangerous branch. Hamilton argued that the federal judiciary posed no serious threat because it had to depend on the other two branches to carry out its decisions. He also noted that the interpretation of laws is a proper function of the courts. Since the Constitution itself is a fundamental law, he concluded that the Supreme Court has the authority to decide its meaning as well as the meaning of particular laws.

The Supreme Court doesn't issue advisory opinions. It handles only disagreements or controversies between two parties over specific issues. It generally acts as an appeals court, reviewing the decisions of other courts. This is called appellate jurisdiction. In some instances, however, the Supreme Court acts as a trial court, hearing evidence and reaching a conclusion. This is called original jurisdiction.

In 1789 the First Congress passed the Judiciary Act to establish the federal court system. The law called for one chief justice and five associate justices on a Supreme Court. It also established several lower federal courts, and gave the Supreme Court specific authority to review the decisions of these courts and state court decisions involving the Constitution or federal laws. In addition, the act gave the Supreme Court the authority to issue orders compelling federal officials to perform their official duties.

In 1803, in the case of *Marbury* v. *Madison*, the Supreme Court affirmed its own authority to interpret the Constitution. The case grew out of a law passed in 1801 in the closing days of the presidency of John Adams, a Federalist. This law increased the number of federal judges and other federal judiciary officers, enabling the outgoing president to appoint a number of his fellow Federalists to these posts. The incoming president, Thomas Jefferson, a Democratic-Republican (the name the Anti-Federalists had adopted), was angry over the appointment of these "midnight judges." When he found that the outgoing secretary of state, John Marshall, had not delivered the commissions to some of the new appointees before leaving office, Jefferson ordered the new secretary of state, James Madison, to withhold delivery of these commissions. William Marbury, who had been appointed a justice of the peace for the District of Columbia, then asked the Supreme Court to order Madison to deliver his appointment papers to him.

The new chief justice, John Marshall, was in a difficult situation. If he ordered Madison to deliver the papers, he had no way of forcing Madison to obey this order. But how could Marshall refuse to take an action for which he had express legal authority? Marshall wiggled out of the tight spot by holding that the section of the Judiciary Act of 1789 that authorized the Supreme Court to issue such an order was unconstitutional because Congress could not give the Court more authority than the Constitution itself gave it. Therefore, the Court had no authority to try to force Madison to deliver the commission to Marbury. Marshall reasoned that a law that conflicts with the Constitution is invalid, and that the Court has the duty to enforce the Constitution by striking down such a law.

In the years following the *Marbury* decision, the Supreme Court has issued numerous rulings that interpret the provisions of the Constitution. Some of these interpretations have changed over time, occasionally resulting in a complete reversal of an earlier ruling, as different justices responded to changing circumstances. A few Supreme Court rulings have resulted in major changes in American society.

Although most Supreme Court decisions have attracted little notice, a few have caused great controversy (including demands for constitutional amendments) either because people thought that the Court was actually amending the Constitution without going through Congress and the states, or because they believed that the Court decision was wrong. Many of the most serious disagreements have involved the Bill of Rights, which was adopted to safeguard our most precious freedoms.

THE BILL OF RIGHTS

The first ten amendments to the Constitution, all adopted in 1791, are commonly known as the Bill of Rights. However, only the first eight amendments protect our individual rights. The other two clarify the rights and powers of the states and the federal government. The purpose of the Bill of Rights is to protect the individual against governmental interference.

> ### THE FIRST AMENDMENT (1791)
> Congress shall make no law respecting an establishment of religion, or prohibiting the free exercise thereof; or abridging the freedom of speech, or of the press; or the right of the people peaceably to assemble, and to petition the Government for a redress of grievances.

The First Amendment protects us in five separate but related areas: freedom of religion, freedom of speech, freedom of the press, freedom of assembly, and the right of petition.

Freedom of Religion
The First Amendment's clause of religious freedom grew out of objections to the European practice of set-

ting up a state church supported by taxes and requiring people to attend its services regardless of their beliefs and wishes. The clause contains both a ban on an establishment of religion and a guarantee of people's right to its free exercise. These two provisions sometimes conflict with one another.

An Establishment of Religion

For many years the Supreme Court had little to say about the ban on an establishment of religion because this provision was applied only to the actions of Congress. It wasn't until the twentieth century that the Court applied the First Amendment to the actions of states. (The Court did so by holding that the Fourteenth Amendment made the Bill of Rights applicable to state as well as federal actions.)

At first the establishment of religion clause was generally interpreted as referring merely to the setting up of an official national church while leaving the government free to aid religious institutions provided it does not favor one religion over another. A more common view today is that the First Amendment erects a wall of separation between church and state (a view held by Thomas Jefferson). This interpretation makes any government support of religion suspect. In 1971 the Supreme Court tried to clarify the question of the constitutionality of government aid to church-related institutions by providing a three-part test for determining whether such aid is constitutional. The Court held that in order to be constitutional the aid must have a valid secular (or nonreligious) purpose, it must neither promote nor hinder religion, and it must avoid an excessive government entanglement with religion. This test has not completely resolved the question. For example, in 1985 the Court ruled that public funds may not be used to allow public school teachers to conduct remedial or enrichment classes for poor children in religious schools. To comply with this decision many teachers held such classes off the school grounds, often in vans or buses parked outside the schools. In June 1997 the Court reversed itself and held that the use of public funds for the teaching of secular subjects in religious schools does not violate the First Amendment's establishment of religion clause.

The Supreme Court has also dealt with such issues as whether the display of religious symbols on public property and the recitation of prayers in public schools are unconstitutional "establishments" of religion. The issue of prayer in public schools, which is discussed in Chapter 14, was and is extremely controversial.

The Free Exercise of Religion

Religious practices that conflict with the government's lawful authority to promote public health, safety, and welfare are not protected by the First Amendment. Balancing the government's legitimate concerns regarding these issues with the rights of individuals to act in accordance with their religious beliefs isn't always easy. The Supreme Court has made a number of decisions in an attempt to clarify this difficult issue.

One of the earliest decisions regarding this issue distinguished between beliefs (which are protected under the First Amendment) and conduct (which isn't necessarily protected). The case dealt with the former practice of many members of the Church of Jesus Christ of Latter-day Saints, commonly known as Mormons, of having more than one wife (a practice called polygamy). In 1878 the Supreme Court upheld a law of the Territory of Utah that prohibited polygamy. In concluding that this law didn't infringe on the Mormons' free exercise of religion, the Court noted that Congress (which administered the territories) has the right to forbid actions that violate social duties or interfere with social order.

In 1940 the Supreme Court upheld a state law compelling public school children to recite the pledge of allegiance to the American flag as part of a daily school ceremony. The case involved children whose families were members of the Jehovah's Witnesses, a religious group that forbade saluting the flag on the grounds that it was really a worship of idols. The Court upheld the compulsory flag-salute law on the grounds that it did not violate the children's right to the free exercise of their religion. Three years later, however, the Court reversed itself. In a case involving nearly identical facts, the Court held that the compulsory flag salute violated the right of free speech. The Court reasoned that the right to free speech includes the right to remain silent when a required statement (the pledge of allegiance) conflicts with one's religious beliefs.

Since that time the Supreme Court's decisions have shifted between upholding people's right to practice their religion and affirming the state's interest in preventing people from breaking a law based on a claim that the law conflicts with their religious beliefs.

Freedom of Speech and the Press

These two closely related provisions of the First Amendment were intended primarily to protect political speech and writings. The sponsors of the amendment wanted to make sure that people were generally free to criticize the government without fear of punishment. They also wanted to prevent the government from censoring printed material before it was published.

In the years following World War II the Supreme Court has greatly expanded the scope of the First Amendment rights of free speech and a free press in two areas. First, it has given some protection to visual art

The claim that the recitation of the Pledge of
Allegiance in public schools was contrary to the
religious practices of some people prompted a number
of Supreme Court cases. Ultimately the Court
determined that to require the Pledge's recitation
violates children's right to free speech, but not
necessarily their freedom of religion.

forms such as paintings, drawings, and motion pictures and to advertising and similar commercial speech. Second, the Court has applied these rights to nonverbal acts of protest such as burning or trampling on the flag or carrying signs or posters. Because of these expanded interpretations of freedom of speech and the press, we often refer to them as freedom of expression.

Generally, the Court has granted First Amendment protection even to offensive speech. However, the Court has carved out exceptions for sexually explicit material (obscenity), for speech that advocates the overthrow of the government and that results in illegal acts (incitement), and for libel (writings that tend to damage a person's reputation) involving criticisms of political or other public figures. The tendency in each of these areas, nevertheless, has been to give them broad protection under the First Amendment.

The rights of free assembly and petition are closely connected to freedom of speech. Freedom of assembly applies to political protests and demonstrations as well as to parades, rallies, and other public activities. Freedom of petition applies to organized efforts to enlist public support for various causes as well as to direct appeals to Congress for changes in federal laws. The First Amendment protects all of these activities, which are often called freedom of association, as long as they are peaceful.

THE SECOND AMENDMENT (1791)

A well regulated Militia, being necessary to the security of a free State, the right of the people to keep and bear Arms, shall not be infringed.

State and local militia units played an important part in the struggle for American independence. When the

Constitution was adopted, many people were afraid that the new central government might replace these groups of citizen soldiers with a national army that could be used to deprive them of their individual rights. They were also accustomed to owning and carrying firearms to protect themselves and their families, and didn't want to give them up. The Second Amendment was a response to both of these concerns.

Although there are many laws regulating and restricting the manufacture and sale of firearms, many Americans, concerned about the widespread availability of increasingly dangerous handguns and their use in violent crimes, want more restrictions on these weapons. Congress has responded to these concerns by enacting stricter gun-control laws in the belief that this is a national problem that state laws alone can't solve. Opponents of these laws, who believe that restrictions on their ability to own guns violate their Second Amendment rights, have challenged them in the federal courts. In the 1990s, the Court has struck down two federal gun-control measures. However, the Court based its decisions on the Tenth Amendment, not the Second.

THE THIRD AMENDMENT (1791)

No Soldier shall, in time of peace be quartered in any house, without the consent of the Owner, nor in time of war, but in a manner to be prescribed by law.

This amendment was adopted to prevent a recurrence of the British practice of housing (or quartering) troops in colonists' homes without their consent. It has little or no practical significance today, since members of the armed forces either live on the grounds of military installations or have housing in nearby communities.

THE FOURTH AMENDMENT (1791)

The right of the people to be secure in their persons, houses, papers, and effects, against unreasonable searches and seizures, shall not be violated, and no Warrants shall issue, but upon probable cause, supported by Oath or affirmation, and particularly describing the place to be searched, and the persons or things to be seized.

This amendment was a reaction to the British practice during the colonial period of searching people's homes for smuggled goods based on "writs of assistance" that didn't specify what the searchers hoped to find.

Not all searches require a search warrant (an official authorization issued by a court for a particular search). For example, a warrant generally is not needed for searches in the course of an arrest or immediately following the pursuit of a suspected criminal, or for the seizure of an object in plain sight even though the warrant doesn't specify it.

Police officers sometimes conduct searches without obtaining a necessary warrant, or go beyond a search warrant's authorization. As a deterrent to this type of conduct the courts have often ruled that evidence obtained illegally may not be used in criminal trials and have overturned convictions based on such evidence. This is called the exclusionary rule. In 1984 the Supreme Court relaxed this rule somewhat by holding that evidence obtained in good faith but later found to be based on a defective warrant can be used in a criminal trial. Both the 1984 decision and the rule itself are controversial. Supporters of the rule argue that it is needed to protect people's Fourth Amendment rights, while opponents point out that it sometimes allows guilty persons to escape punishment.

THE FIFTH AMENDMENT (1791)

No person shall be held to answer for a capital, or otherwise infamous crime, unless on a presentment or indictment of a Grand Jury, except in cases arising in the land or naval forces, or in the Militia, when in actual service in time of War or public danger; nor shall any person be subject for the same offense to be twice put in jeopardy of life or limb; nor shall be compelled in any criminal case to be a witness against himself, nor be deprived of life, liberty, or property, without due process of law; nor shall private property be taken for public use without just compensation.

This important amendment protects people who have been accused of crimes. It also contains safeguards that protect the general public.

The Fifth Amendment requirement of a grand-jury indictment protects people from being tried for criminal offenses without enough evidence of wrongdoing to justify putting them on trial. The ban on double jeopardy means that a person who has been found not guilty of a crime cannot be tried again in the same court system for the same crime. He can, however, be tried by a court in another jurisdiction. For example, a person who has been acquitted in a state court can be tried for the same offense in a federal court.

The right of persons not to be witnesses against themselves means that they do not have to give information that might implicate them in criminal activities. Information that persons give voluntarily, including confessions of guilt, can be used against them in court, but only if they have been warned about the possibility of such use and informed of their right not to answer questions.

The term "due process of law" is not defined in the Constitution. In criminal cases it generally means that persons cannot receive criminal penalties without first having been found guilty in a court of law. The requirement of due process also applies in many cases that do not involve the commission of a crime. For example, benefits that people receive under various government programs, such as Social Security and Medicare (health benefits for the elderly and disabled) are considered property. The payment of these benefits may not be stopped without giving the recipient advance notice and an opportunity to show why the benefits should be continued.

The provision of the Fifth Amendment regarding the taking of private property refers to the government's right to condemn property (declare that it is needed for public use). This right is called eminent domain. When the government takes property for public use, the Fifth Amendment requires that the owner receive a fair price for it. Changes in statutes that restrict the way property may be used, such as zoning laws that designate certain areas for business, industrial, or residential use, do not generally require compensation because of the changes. However, the Supreme Court has ruled that changes that make property worthless require that the owner be compensated for the loss. For example, a law prohibiting any further building on expensive beachfront property may make the property worthless and thus require that its owner be compensated for the financial loss.

THE SIXTH AMENDMENT (1791)

In all criminal prosecutions, the accused shall enjoy the right to a speedy and public trial, by an impartial jury of the State and district wherein the crime shall have been committed, which district shall have been previously ascertained by law, and to be informed of the nature and cause of the accusation; to be confronted with the witnesses against him; to have compulsory process for obtaining Witnesses in his favor, and to have the assistance of counsel for his defence.

During the colonial period, Americans viewed the right to trial by jury as an important protection against arbitrary decisions by government officials. They also remembered Great Britain's past practice of keeping political opponents in prison for long periods without charging them with any crime and of holding secret trials based on the evidence of unidentified witnesses. The Sixth Amendment responded to all these concerns.

The right to have the assistance of legal counsel originally meant simply the right to hire a lawyer to help in a person's defense. It now includes the right of a person who is unable to pay a lawyer's fees to have the help of a court-appointed lawyer.

The Sixth Amendment right to legal counsel is closely related to the Fifth Amendment right not to incriminate oneself. In a landmark 1966 decision (*Miranda* v. *Arizona*) the Supreme Court ruled that before a suspect in police custody can be questioned, he must be told that any information he gives during questioning can be used against him in court, and that he has the right to refuse to answer questions and to have a lawyer present during questioning. If he doesn't have a lawyer or can't afford to hire one, he must be given the assistance of a court-appointed lawyer before any questions are asked. Unless these procedures are followed, no evidence obtained during police questioning can be used against a person in a criminal trial. Despite a widespread outcry from law enforcement officials at the time, the changes mandated by this decision have generally not resulted in major disruptions of criminal prosecutions.

THE SEVENTH AMENDMENT (1791)
In Suits at common law, where the value in controversy shall exceed twenty dollars, the right of trial by jury shall

be preserved, and no fact tried by a jury, shall be otherwise re-examined in any Court of the United States, than according to the rules of the common law.

This amendment extends the right of a jury trial to civil lawsuits as well as criminal cases. Some Anti-Federalists had argued that the Constitution might abolish jury trials in civil suits. They also warned that even if such trials continued, appeals to the federal courts might result in the reopening of the entire case and the reversal of the jury's decisions. To guard against this possibility the amendment bans the federal courts from reopening the case and reaching their own conclusion regarding the facts. The twenty-dollar figure, which is outdated today, was a considerable amount of money when the amendment was adopted.

THE EIGHTH AMENDMENT (1791)
Excessive bail shall not be required, nor excessive fines imposed, nor cruel and unusual punishments inflicted.

The Eighth Amendment was intended to prevent courts from imposing unreasonable financial burdens on persons accused of crimes, and torture or other forms of punishment that were considered barbarous. Today the ban on cruel and unusual punishment comes up most often regarding the death penalty.

When the Bill of Rights was adopted, the death penalty was neither unusual nor regarded as particularly cruel. Public hangings of convicted criminals often took on a holiday atmosphere, with people traveling long distances to witness the spectacle. Given the prevailing attitude at the time, it is doubtful that the First Congress considered the death penalty as either cruel or unusual.

The modern crusade against the death penalty is closely tied to the civil-rights movement. The National Association for the Advancement of Colored People, aware that blacks were far more likely to be sentenced to death than whites, challenged the death penalty as a violation of both the Eighth Amendment's ban on cruel and unusual punishment and the people's right to due process of law. In 1972 the Supreme Court held that as it was administered the death penalty violated both constitutional provisions. The Court was divided on this issue, however. The justices were split five to four on the decision itself, and issued nine separate opinions.

In 1976 the Court issued two more decisions regarding the death penalty. One held that mandatory death sentences violate the Eighth Amendment because they don't give judges and juries the flexibility to consider individual circumstances. The other decision upheld a Georgia law that provided for an examination of both mitigating and aggravating circumstances before a death sentence could be imposed. Mitigating circumstances are those that might call for a less severe punishment, such as the guilty person's age, mental condition, or lack of a previous criminal record. Aggravating circumstances, which make a crime more heinous, include its commission while engaged in another serious crime, such as a rape and murder, or its extremely brutal nature, such as a murder committed after torturing or mutilating the victim. Most state laws today, if they allow the death penalty, provide similar guidelines.

Another frequent question regarding the Eighth Amendment is whether the treatment of prison inmates constitutes cruel and unusual punishment. Prisoners often file lawsuits claiming they are receiving cruel and unusual punishment over seemingly trivial issues, such as their right to have things that make prison life more comfortable. However, some of these suits deal with significant problems, such as beatings and other inhumane treatment at the hands of prison personnel.

THE NINTH AMENDMENT (1791)
The enumeration in the Constitution, of certain rights, shall not be construed to deny or disparage others retained by the people.

This provision was added because of concerns that the listing of specific rights in the Constitution might imply that those not listed were not granted. It is often used today to justify rulings that affirm constitutional rights that the Constitution doesn't mention. For example, in several decisions during the 1960s and 1970s the Supreme Court held that the Bill of Rights gives Americans a constitutional right of privacy.

THE TENTH AMENDMENT (1791)
The powers not delegated to the United States by the Constitution, nor prohibited by it to the States, are reserved to the States respectively, or to the people.

This amendment was added in response to the arguments of the Anti-Federalists that the Constitution, by giving so much power to the central government, would destroy the independence of the states. The amendment is ambiguous, however. Although it may have given some comfort to advocates of states' rights, it has often been used to justify the federal government's assumption of powers not expressly given to it in the Constitution—the so-called implied powers of Congress. The original Constitution gives Congress broad powers in certain designated areas, such as the powers to tax and spend for the common defense and the general welfare and to regulate interstate commerce. Various amendments have increased these powers. However, from time to time the Supreme Court has reminded Congress that although its powers are broad, they are not unlimited. In 1995, for example, the Court, by a five-to-four majority, struck down a 1990 federal law that made it a crime to have a gun in or near a school. The law, like many laws involving criminal justice, was based on Congress's power to regulate interstate commerce. For more than fifty years the Court had interpreted this power broadly. In ruling on the 1990 law, however, the Court gave a narrower interpretation of the commerce clause. Chief Justice William Rehnquist, speaking for the majority, held that a restriction on the possession of guns on school property has no relation to interstate commerce, and thus the 1990 law was unconstitutional. Similarly, in another five-to-four decision, the Court ruled in 1997 that Congress cannot compel state and local officials to check the backgrounds of persons who want to buy handguns to determine whether they are barred from buying them under a 1993 federal law. The Court said that Congress can ask the states to conduct the checks voluntarily or can grant federal funds for this activity, but the law as written unconstitutionally violated states' rights.

TWO EARLY AMENDMENTS

Not long after the ratification of the Bill of Rights, two more amendments were added to the Constitution. The Eleventh and Twelfth Amendments were adopted to correct constitutional language that produced undesirable results. The Eleventh Amendment was also a reaction to an unpopular Supreme Court decision.

THE ELEVENTH AMENDMENT (1795)
The Judicial power of the United States shall not be construed to extend to any suit in law or equity, commenced or prosecuted against one of the United States by Citizens of another State, or by Citizens or Subjects of any Foreign State.

The fears of the Anti-Federalists that the powers given by the Constitution to the federal courts would destroy the authority of the states was reinforced by a provision that seemed to allow individuals to file lawsuits against states in the Supreme Court. The Federalists insisted that the Anti-Federalists' fears were mistaken because states couldn't be sued without their permission—a doctrine called sovereign immunity. In 1793 the Supreme Court made a decision that indicated that the

Anti-Federalists' interpretation of the Constitution regarding that Court's jurisdiction was right.

Chisholm *v.* Georgia

Robert Farquar, a resident of Charleston, South Carolina, died in 1784. At the time of his death, Farquar was trying to collect money for supplies he had delivered to American troops at Savannah, Georgia, in 1777, as authorized by two Georgia state commissioners. The state apparently had given its commissioners the money to pay Farquar, but they never turned it over to him. When Alexander Chisholm, the executor of Farquar's estate, asked the Georgia legislature to pay this debt, that body refused and advised Chisholm to look to the two commissioners for payment of the debt. Instead, Chisholm filed suit against Georgia in a lower federal court. After the court ruled against him, Chisholm then took the case to the U.S. Supreme Court.[1]

The suit was filed with the Supreme Court in accordance with Article III, Section 2 of the Constitution, which provided that the federal judicial power extended to the cases involving controversies "between a State and Citizens of another State" or between a state and citizens or subjects of a foreign country. It provided further that the Supreme Court had original jurisdiction—that is, it acted as a trial court—over all cases in which a state was a party to the lawsuit. Georgia, believing that as a sovereign state—that is, an entity not under the control of another government—it could not be sued by individuals, took no part in the arguments on this case other than to claim that the Supreme Court lacked jurisdiction over it.

On February 18, 1793, the justices announced their decisions. All of them except Justice James Iredell of North Carolina, who had been a delegate to that state's ratifying convention, agreed that the Supreme Court had jurisdiction over the case. Justice James Wilson (who had read Benjamin Franklin's speech on the last day of the constitutional convention) delivered a resounding lecture on the question of whether a state could be sued in a federal court. As Wilson saw it, the real issue was Georgia's status as a sovereign power. He declared that sovereignty (the power to govern) rested in the people, not the states. Wilson then stated that it was repugnant to the very existence of the United States as a nation to allow any state to exempt itself from the national government's jurisdiction. He asserted: "As to the purposes of the Union, therefore, Georgia is not a sovereign state."[2]

The Court's decision set off a national furor. The outcry was due as much to practical economic considerations as to political philosophy. The *Chisholm* decision opened the door to many other Supreme Court cases involving individuals who believed that a state owed them money. A few such suits were filed right after the Supreme Court announced its decision in *Chisholm*. Georgia was especially outraged by the decision. The lower house of the Georgia legislature promptly passed a bill making it a crime punishable by hanging for any federal official to try to enforce the Court's decision. The bill did not become law, however.

The Response of Congress and the States

It didn't take long for both the state legislatures and Congress to act. Virginia and Massachusetts called special sessions of their state legislatures, which urged Congress to pass a constitutional amendment. Congress was ahead of the states, however: The first resolution calling for a constitutional amendment was introduced in Congress the day after the Supreme Court announced its decision.

In 1996, the Supreme Court decided that it was unconstitutional for American Indian tribes to sue their state governments for the right to operate casinos on their reservations. This decision was based on the Eleventh Amendment, which hadn't been cited in the Supreme Court in many years.

On March 4, 1794, Congress passed the Eleventh Amendment. Less than a year later, on February 7, 1795, it was added to the Constitution after North Carolina became the twelfth state to ratify it. The amendment requires lawsuits against states by citizens of another state or a foreign country to be filed in state courts instead of federal courts. The federal courts, however, can review state court decisions in suits filed against the states in cases involving the Constitution or a federal law.

Georgia was never forced to pay anything as a result of the *Chisholm* case, although it did eventually pay its debt to Farquar's survivors. In 1789 a unanimous Supreme Court held that because of the adoption of the Eleventh Amendment it had no jurisdiction over any past or present cases in which a state was sued by citizens of another state or foreign country.

For many years the Eleventh Amendment seemed to be an outdated provision that no longer had much relevance. It returned to public notice in 1996, however, when the Supreme Court struck down a federal law that allowed American Indian tribes to sue state governments in federal courts over their right to allow gambling on their reservations. The Court based its decision on the Eleventh Amendment, which prevents "Citizens," in this instance the Seminole Indians, from suing a state in a federal court.

THE TWELFTH AMENDMENT (1804)

The electors shall meet in their respective states and vote by ballot for President and Vice-President, one of whom, at least, shall not be an inhabitant of the same state with themselves; they shall name in their ballots the person voted for as President, and in distinct ballots the person voted for as

Vice-President, and they shall make distinct lists of all persons voted for as President, and of all persons voted for as Vice-President, and of the number of votes for each, which lists they shall sign and certify, and transmit sealed to the seat of the government of the United States, directed to the President of the Senate; —The President of the Senate shall, in the presence of the Senate and House of Representatives, open all the certificates and the votes shall then be counted; —The person having the greatest number of votes for President, shall be the President, if such number be a majority of the whole number of Electors appointed; and if no person have such majority, then from the persons having the highest numbers not exceeding three on the list of those voted for as President, the House of Representatives shall choose immediately, by ballot, the President. But in choosing the President, the votes shall be taken by states, the representation from each state having one vote; a quorum for this purpose shall consist of a member or members from two-thirds of the states, and a majority of all the states shall be necessary to a choice.

And if the House of Representatives shall not choose a President whenever the right of choice shall devolve upon them, before the fourth day of March next following, then the Vice-President shall act as President, as in the case of the death or other constitutional disability of the President. The person having the greatest number of votes as Vice-President, shall be the Vice-President, if such a number be a majority of the whole number of Electors appointed, and if no person have a majority, then from the two highest numbers on the list, the Senate shall choose the Vice-President; a quorum for the purpose shall consist of two-thirds of the whole number of Senators, and a majority of the whole number shall be necessary to a choice. But no person constitutionally ineligible to the office of President shall be eligible to that of Vice-President of the United States.

The Electoral College

The delegates to the 1787 constitutional convention disagreed on who should choose the president. Many favored giving the choice to Congress. Others favored a direct election by the voters of the entire country. The idea of having a group of presidential electors (called an electoral college) choose the president was a middle ground between the other two methods.

The convention agreed to have an electoral college vote for both the president and vice president, with the House of Representatives making the final decision if the electors either tied in their choice or failed to produce a majority vote for any one person. Actually, the delegates thought that the House would make the final selection for these offices in most cases because the electors would tend to vote for many different persons, thus lessening the likelihood of achieving a majority vote.

The Constitution gives each state a number of electors equal to the number of its congressional representatives (that is, its members in the Senate and House combined), and forbids members of Congress or other federal officeholders from serving as presidential electors. Each state legislature decides how to choose these electors, who are to meet in their own states to cast their votes on a date set by Congress.

The Constitution originally provided that the electors would each vote for two persons for the offices of president and vice president. The person receiving the largest number of votes would be elected president, and the person receiving the next highest number would become vice president. At first, things went as the framers of the Constitution expected. In February 1789 each of the sixty-nine electors voted for George Washington, who became our first president. John Adams of Massachusetts, who had recently returned home after ten years in France as the American minister

(49)

to that country, was elected vice president with thirty-four electoral votes. In 1792, Washington and Adams were reelected. So far, so good—but not for long.

The 1796 Election

By 1796 the loose alliance of Anti-Federalists had organized into a political party. These men, who now called themselves Democratic-Republicans, named Thomas Jefferson as their candidate for president against John Adams, the Federalist candidate. (Washington had declined to run for a third term as president.) The vote was close—seventy-one votes for Adams and sixty-eight for Jefferson. That made Adams president and Jefferson, his political opponent, vice president. That wasn't quite what the framers of the Constitution had intended. People began to call for a constitutional amendment. Not much happened, however, until after the 1800 election.

The 1800 Election

By 1800 the two political parties had developed to the point where they not only chose their own teams of candidates for president and vice president but also backed the selection of electors who pledged to vote for these men. The Democratic-Republicans once again chose Jefferson as their presidential candidate. Aaron Burr of New York was their choice for vice president. The Federalist candidates were Adams and Charles C. Pinckney of South Carolina.

The Federalists had become unpopular by 1800. As a result, a majority of the electoral college members chosen in that year's election were Democratic-Republicans. That meant that Jefferson should have been elected president with Burr as his vice president. But something went wrong. Instead of making sure that Jefferson got at least one more vote than Burr, the electors split their votes evenly between the two men. The fact that the electors voted in sixteen different locations (one for each state) may have contributed to the difficulty of arranging ahead of time how to split their votes. At any rate, Jefferson and Burr each received seventy-three electoral votes, while Adams came in third with sixty-five votes. This meant that it would be up to the House of Representatives to choose Jefferson or Burr as the next president. To make matters worse, the Federalists had a majority in the House when it voted for president early in 1801. The new Congress, which would have a majority of Democratic-Republicans, wouldn't take office for several months. The Federalist members of the House couldn't vote for Adams, their candidate, because the Constitution required them to choose between the two who tied in electoral votes. Many of them preferred Burr to Jefferson.

The Constitution provided that when the House of Representatives chose the president, each state would have one vote. The initial vote in the House resulted in a tie—eight states for Jefferson and eight for Burr. Subsequent voting had the same result. It went on and on, ballot after ballot. The voting dragged on so long that some people began to wonder whether the country would have a president on March 4, 1801, the date the newly elected president was to take office. Finally the House adjourned over a weekend to do some behind-the-scenes negotiating. Alexander Hamilton, who disliked Burr, may have influenced these negotiations. When the House resumed voting, Jefferson got the votes of ten states—one more than he needed to be elected president. Burr became vice president.

Congress Acts to Remedy the Situation

After the House finally settled the election, a constitutional amendment to require separate electoral voting for president and vice president was introduced in Congress. To avoid a repeat of the uncertainty over who would be president if the House failed to elect someone before the new president was due to take office, the amendment also provided that in such an event the vice president would become president until the election was decided. On December 9, 1803, close to three years after Jefferson's election, Congress passed the Twelfth Amendment. It became part of the Constitution on June 15, 1804, so that the new rules applied to the 1804 presidential election. Jefferson won that election easily over his Federalist opponent, Charles C. Pinckney of South Carolina. Jefferson's new vice president was George Clinton of New York. By that time Burr had quarreled with Jefferson over political matters. Moreover, Burr's political career was ruined after he killed Alexander Hamilton in a duel on July 11, 1804.

After the adoption of the Twelfth Amendment, more than sixty years passed before the Constitution was amended again. The next amendments came only after the end of a four-year civil war during which the survival of the Union was at stake.

AN END TO SLAVERY

The Thirteenth, Fourteenth, and Fifteenth Amendments were all enacted shortly after the Civil War and had as their primary purpose the elimination of slavery and the guarantee of equal treatment for freed slaves.

THE THIRTEENTH AMENDMENT (1865)

SECTION 1. Neither slavery nor involuntary servitude, except as a punishment for crime whereof the party shall have been duly convicted, shall exist in the United States, or any place subject to their jurisdiction.

SECTION 2. Congress shall have power to enforce this article by appropriate legislation.

Slavery, which had existed in America since the early colonial period, divided Americans throughout much of our early history. The controversy over slavery, along with other issues, eventually threatened the Union's very existence, and it was finally ended only after the Civil War and the adoption of a constitutional amendment.

SLAVERY—
A DYING INSTITUTION?

By the time the constitutional convention met in 1787, slavery appeared to be dying out in America. The gradual change from an agricultural to an industrial economy in the northern states made the practice unprofitable. Several of these states took action to abolish slavery either immediately or on a gradual basis. Moreover, while the convention was meeting in Philadelphia, Congress passed a law forbidding slavery in the Northwest Territory, which later became the states of Ohio, Indiana, Illinois, Michigan, and Wisconsin.

There was reason to believe that slavery would eventually end in the South, too. In 1787 slaves were used mainly on tobacco plantations. This industry was declining, making it seem likely that slavery would eventually become unprofitable in the South as well. This belief turned out to be wrong, however. The invention in 1793 of the cotton gin, a machine that removed the seeds from cotton, made cotton-growing profitable. As a result, instead of dying out, slavery became an important part of the South's economy.

There were moral as well as economic reasons to oppose slavery when the Constitution was being formed. By the end of the Revolutionary War, some Americans had begun to question the morality of one person's ownership of another in a country that claimed to value individual freedom. A fair number of northern delegates to the 1787 convention and a few from the slave-owning states in the South shared this viewpoint. The majority of the delegates believed, however, that their job was to strengthen and preserve the Union, not to debate the morality or immorality of slavery. They therefore made the compromises on slavery discussed in Chapter 1 to get the southern states to ratify the Constitution. No one suggested that the national government should be given the power to control or end slavery within a state's borders. This was considered a matter for the states themselves to handle. Antislavery delegates had to be content with the hope that the states that still allowed slavery would abolish it themselves.

SLAVERY IN THE TERRITORIES

Slavery in the territories was another matter. Article IV of the Constitution gives Congress the power to make all needful rules and regulations respecting territories or other property belonging to the United States. Presumably this included the power to regulate or abolish slavery. As the United States expanded its geographical area, the question of slavery in the territories led to many controversies. To resolve them Congress made several compromises in an effort to preserve the fragile bonds that held the nation together.

THE MISSOURI COMPROMISE

The first congressional compromise occurred after Missouri, which was part of the Louisiana Purchase (the land that President Jefferson bought from France in 1803), applied for admission as a state in 1819. At that time there were eleven slave states (states that allowed slavery) and eleven free states (states that forbade slavery) in the Union. Many political leaders in both the North and the South thought it was important to maintain an even distribution of Senate seats between the two sections to prevent one section from obtaining domination over the other. The admission of Missouri, which allowed slavery, would upset the balance by giving the slave states two more votes in the Senate than the free states.

Actually, the balance had shifted back and forth several times in the past as new states were admitted. The admission of Missouri might not have caused such a great controversy had it not been for two factors: a northern antislavery representative's proposal that, as a condition for admission, slaves be barred from entering the new state and children born to slave women be freed on reaching age twenty-five; and the possibility that Missouri's admission as a slave state might open the door to slavery in the entire area gained in the Louisiana Purchase.

The dispute was resolved after Maine, which was then part of Massachusetts, applied for admission as a separate state. Maine's admission as a free state in 1820 allowed Congress to admit Missouri as a slave state the following year, thus restoring the balance of senate seats. Congress also tried to prevent future disputes regarding the Louisiana Purchase by banning slavery in the parts that lay north of Missouri's southern border (36° 30' north latitude), but leaving the door open to the admission of slave states south of that line. The Missouri Compromise postponed the need to deal with the controversial issue of the expansion of slavery into the territories—but not for very long.

THE ADMISSION OF TEXAS AND THE MEXICAN CESSION

The admission of Texas as the fifteenth slave state in December 1845 (which was in itself a controversial event) and the subsequent war with Mexico greatly increased the North-South tensions over slavery. The admission of Texas further upset the balance between slave and free states, already tilted in favor of the slave states by Florida's admission as the twenty-seventh state in March 1845, which made a total of fourteen slave states and thirteen free states. Moreover, the terms under which Texas was admitted allowed it to be divided into five states, all of which were likely to permit slavery. That was bad enough, but things got worse after the Mexican War ended. Under the 1848 peace treaty with Mexico the United States gained a huge expanse of territory, called the Mexican Cession, that stretched all the way to the Pacific Ocean. The question of how much of the territory would be open to slavery came up almost immediately.

The Compromise of 1850

California's application for admission to the Union as a free state brought matters to a head. The admission of California would again upset the balance between free and slave states, which had been restored by the admission of Iowa and Wisconsin as free states, making a total of fifteen free states and fifteen slave states. During the debate over the admission of California, some northerners demanded that it be admitted promptly as a free state, while some southerners called for the disbanding of the Union if that should happen.

Senator Henry Clay of Kentucky, a member of the Whig party, drafted several proposals for settling the dispute. (Clay, who worked out many compromises to settle political disputes, became known as the Great Compromiser.) Senator Stephen A. Douglas, an Illinois Democrat, pushed Clay's proposals through Congress in a series of separate bills. One bill admitted California as a free state. Another allowed the residents of the rest of the Mexican Cession—the Utah and New Mexico Territories—to organize territorial governments with no stipulations regarding slavery, leaving them free to decide for themselves whether to allow it. This was called popular sovereignty. Once again, a catastrophe had been averted. Southern talk of disbanding the Union stopped. The Union was safe— for the time being.

THE KANSAS-NEBRASKA CONTROVERSY

In 1853, Senator Douglas introduced a bill to organize a government for the Nebraska Territory (which was part of the Louisiana Purchase of 1803) so that a railroad could be built through that area. In accordance with the Missouri Compromise, slavery would be forbidden in the newly organized territory. After southern senators defeated the bill, Douglas introduced a new bill dividing the area into two territories (Nebraska and Kansas) and providing for popular sovereignty in both territories instead of making them "free soil" as required by the Missouri Compromise. The passage of the Kansas-Nebraska Act in 1854 caused an immediate uproar in the North. Northerners complained about a slave power conspiracy to force slavery on the whole country. Their outrage increased when open civil war broke out in Kansas between slave owners and abolitionists. Two rival governments were formed, and terrorism was rampant. Soon the slogan "Bleeding Kansas" seemed to be on everyone's lips.

THE FORMATION OF THE REPUBLICAN PARTY

Northerners who opposed the spread of slavery into the newly organized territories formed political alliances that resulted in the formation of a new political party, the Republican party. The new party's main goal was to stop the further expansion of slavery. In 1856 the party's presidential candidate, John C. Frémont, lost the election to the Democratic candidate, James Buchanan, but

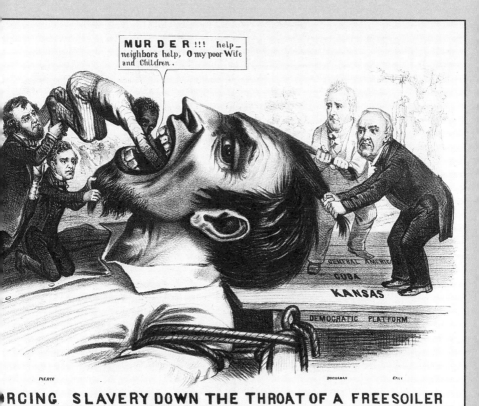

RCING SLAVERY DOWN THE THROAT OF A FREESOILER

The Kansas-Nebraska Act of 1854 caused an
immediate uproar in the northern states. Rather
than make the Nebraska territory "free soil," as
called for in the Missouri Compromise, it was split
into two territories, Nebraska and Kansas.
Popular sovereignty would decide the slavery
question. Many felt that slavery was being "shoved
down the throats" of the people who lived in the
territories, as this cartoon implies.

(59)

the Republicans resolved to try again in four years. By that time the Whig party was on the verge of complete collapse, and the Democrats, although winners in 1856, were severely damaged.

The Dred Scott Decision

In 1857, shortly after Buchanan's inauguration as president, the Supreme Court issued a decision that many hoped would finally settle the dispute over slavery in the territories. The case involved Dred Scott, a slave who had been taken by his owner to the Wisconsin Territory, a part of the Louisiana Territory that prohibited slavery in accordance with the Missouri Compromise. Scott argued that his residence in free territory made him free. Seven of the nine justices disagreed, ruling that Scott was still a slave.

If the Court had stopped there, its decision might not have caused much of a stir. Chief Justice Roger B. Taney went much further, however. He declared that Scott not only was still a slave, but that blacks, whether slaves or free, could never be American citizens. He also said that Congress had no authority to outlaw slavery in any territory because it could not forbid slave owners from taking their property wherever they chose. Taney's statement, which invalidated both the Missouri Compromise and the doctrine of popular sovereignty, greatly widened the gap between North and South regarding slavery.

THE ELECTION OF LINCOLN AND THE SECESSION CRISIS

The election of 1860 resulted in a complete break in the bonds that had held the Union together up to that point. After the Republican candidate, Abraham Lincoln, was elected president without winning a single southern state, seven southern states seceded (withdrew) from the Union. Congress, alarmed at the prospect of a permanent breakup of the Union, engaged in frantic efforts to coax the seceding states back, or at least to prevent further departures. One such effort was the passage of a constitutional amendment that would have permanently protected slavery in the states where it existed. The amendment passed both houses of Congress by a bare two-thirds majority shortly before Lincoln's inauguration. Although three states ratified the 1861 amendment, the Confederate attack on Fort Sumter in April of that year and the ensuing Civil War ended its chances for becoming part of the Constitution.

THE CIVIL WAR AND SLAVERY

Lincoln's initial aim in fighting the war was to preserve the Union, not to end slavery. Although Lincoln thought slavery was wrong, he believed that Congress had no authority to abolish it in any of the states. He gradually came around to the view that he could defeat the South and preserve the Union only by freeing the slaves.

The Emancipation Proclamation

On January 1, 1863, Lincoln issued the Emancipation Proclamation, which declared that the slaves in areas still in rebellion were free. He justified it as a war measure intended to deprive the South of the use of this valuable human resource. It is doubtful whether his edict actually freed a single slave because it applied only to slaves in the parts of the Confederate states that were not already occupied by Union troops. It had a far more important effect for the long term, however. It made the war a fight to end slavery, not simply to save the Union.

CONGRESS PASSES THE
THIRTEENTH AMENDMENT

The Emancipation Proclamation was a useful weapon against the South during the war, but it wasn't a permanent solution to the problem of slavery. In April 1864 the Senate approved a proposed amendment abolishing slavery throughout the Union, but in June of that year the proposal failed to gain the necessary two-thirds vote in the House. At the end of January 1865 the House voted again on the amendment. This time it was approved by scarcely more than a two-thirds majority. It then went to the states for ratification.

Most northerners believed that the eleven Confederate states had no constitutional right to secede. They were, therefore, still in the Union, which consisted of thirty-six states. Twenty-seven of them had to ratify the Thirteenth Amendment to make it a part of the Constitution. This was impossible without the favorable votes of at least two of the former Confederate states. Andrew Johnson, who became president in April 1865 after Lincoln's death, pressured these states to ratify the amendment as part of the price for readmission of their representatives into Congress. His efforts paid off on December 6, 1865, when Georgia ratified the amendment, making it part of the Constitution.

BADGES AND INCIDENTS OF SLAVERY

The Republicans in Congress recognized that something more than the mere elimination of slavery as a legal relationship was needed if the slaves were to be truly free. The actions of the former Confederate states confirmed their belief that a federal law was needed to enforce the Thirteenth Amendment. The provisional governments established in the South under President

Johnson's authority passed laws that severely restricted the rights of the former slaves. Many northerners thought that these laws, called Black Codes, were really attempts to bring back slavery. In 1866, Congress passed the Civil Rights Act to counteract the effects of the Black Codes and spell out the meaning of the Thirteenth Amendment.

In introducing the bill in the Senate, Senator Lyman Trumbull of Illinois said that it was intended to give effect to the Thirteenth Amendment by securing practical freedom for all. The law, which was passed over President Johnson's veto, made it clear that the freed slaves were American citizens. It also guaranteed their right to make contracts, start lawsuits, testify in court, buy and sell property, and have the same legal protections as whites. The law gave the federal government broad powers to enforce these rights.

In 1968, more than a hundred years after the passage of the 1866 Civil Rights Act, the Supreme Court upheld this law as a valid enforcement of the Thirteenth Amendment. In a unanimous decision in the case of *Jones* v. *Mayer Co.*, the Court held that a property owner's refusal to sell a house to a black purchaser solely because of his race violated the Civil Rights Act of 1866. The Court held that the 1866 law was a legitimate exercise of Congress's power under the Thirteenth Amendment to abolish all "badges and incidents of slavery." In reaching its conclusion the Court ruled that these badges and incidents included any restraint on the ability of blacks to buy and sell property solely because of the color of their skin. As the Court put it, the Thirteenth Amendment would be a mere paper guarantee if Congress did not have the power to assure that a dollar in the hands of a black man will purchase the same thing as a dollar in the hands of a white man. The Court concluded: "At the very least, the freedom that

Congress is empowered to secure under the Thirteenth Amendment includes the freedom to buy whatever a white man can buy, the right to live wherever a white man can live. If Congress cannot say that being a free man means at least this much, then the Thirteenth Amendment made a promise the Nation cannot keep."[3]

CIVIL RIGHTS
AND THE
FOURTEENTH AMENDMENT

THE FOURTEENTH AMENDMENT (1868)

SECTION 1. All persons born or naturalized in the United States, and subject to the jurisdiction thereof, are citizens of the United States and of the State wherein they reside. No State shall make or enforce any law which shall abridge the privileges and immunities of citizens of the United States; nor shall any State deprive any person of life, liberty, or property, without due process of law; nor deny to any person within its jurisdiction the equal protection of the laws.

SECTION 2. Representatives shall be apportioned among the several States according to their respective numbers, counting the whole number of persons in each State, excluding Indians not taxed. But when the right to vote at any election for the choice of electors for President and Vice President of the United States, Representatives in Congress, the Executive and Judicial officers of a State, or the members of the Legislature thereof, is denied to any of the male inhabitants of such state, being twenty-one years of age, and citizens of the United States, or in any way abridged, except for participation in rebellion, or other crime, the basis of representation therein shall be reduced in the proportion which the number of such male citizens shall bear to the whole number of male citizens twenty-one years of age in such State.

SECTION 3. No person shall be a Senator or Representative in Congress, or elector of President and Vice President, or hold any office, civil or military, under the United States, or under any State, who, having previously taken an oath, as a member of Congress, or as a member of any State legislature, or as an executive or judicial officer of any State, to support the Constitution of the United States, shall have engaged in insurrection or rebellion against the same, or given aid and comfort to the enemies thereof. But Congress may by a vote of two-thirds of each House, remove such disability.

SECTION 4. The validity of the public debt of the United States, authorized by law, including debts incurred for payment of pensions and bounties for services in suppressing insurrection or rebellion, shall not be questioned. But neither the United States nor any State shall assume or pay any debt or obligation incurred in aid of insurrection or rebellion against the United States, or any claim for the loss or emancipation of any slave; but all such debts, obligations and claims shall be held illegal and void.

SECTION 5. The Congress shall have power to enforce, by appropriate legislation, the provisions of this article.

The Fourteenth Amendment seemed destined for controversy from the outset. It was born out of a bitter battle between the president and Congress over the treatment of the defeated South after the Civil War—a battle that resulted in the impeachment of the president and a narrow escape from removal from office. It was ratified only after Congress insisted that the southern states accept it as the price for ending military rule and restoring them to their former place in the Union. Nor did the controversies end there. After the Fourteenth Amendment became part of the Constitution, the federal courts reached differing and sometimes conflicting decisions regarding its effects.

THE BATTLE BETWEEN ANDREW JOHNSON AND CONGRESS

Relations between President Andrew Johnson and Congress began to deteriorate soon after the Thirty-Ninth Congress convened in December 1865. In his message to the new Congress, Johnson urged it to seat the newly elected members from the former Confederate states to complete the restoration of these states to their full place in the Union. The heavily Republican Congress had other ideas, however. It refused to seat the newly elected southerners, many of whom had held high rank in the Confederate armed forces or civil government. The congressional Republicans acted out of a belief that the loyalty of these men was doubtful and a recognition that their admission would lessen Republican power in Congress, since the Republican party was virtually nonexistent in the South.

There was a long-range problem, too. The adoption of the Thirteenth Amendment made the Three-Fifths Compromise obsolete. The freeing of the slaves would increase the South's future political power, since these people would now count in the apportionment of seats in the House of Representatives. The next census (1870) would probably give the South more seats in the House. This in turn would mean more southern members in the electoral college, increasing the possibility that a coalition of northern Democrats and southerners would elect a southern president.

Relations between the president and Congress further deteriorated in February 1866, when the president vetoed a bill to extend the life of the Freedmen's Bureau (which had been set up in March 1865 to help the former slaves adjust to their new freedom) and to give it greater powers to carry out its job. Congress later passed another Freedmen's Bureau Act over Johnson's veto.

The president's veto of the Civil Rights Act of 1866, which he condemned as an unconstitutional invasion of states' rights and a step toward concentrating all legislative powers in the federal government, convinced most congressional Republicans that a constitutional amendment was necessary to provide permanent protection for black Americans in the South and to prevent former Confederates from regaining and even increasing their political power at the Republicans' expense.

CONGRESS PASSES
THE FOURTEENTH AMENDMENT

On April 30, 1866, a joint House-Senate committee recommended a constitutional amendment that addressed all of the Republicans' concerns. It acknowledged that black Americans are citizens and forbade the states from infringing on their constitutional rights. It guaranteed the payment of the Union war debt and forbade the payment of both the Confederate debt and any compensation to slave owners for the loss of their slaves. It provided for a reduction in the House membership of any state that denied voting rights to any of its adult male citizens except as a punishment for a crime. It also barred those who had voluntarily aided the Confederacy from voting in national elections until 1870. The Senate removed this provision and substituted one that barred certain former Confederates from holding national or state office unless Congress removed this restriction. On June 13, 1866, Congress passed the Fourteenth Amendment along strict party lines—not a single Democrat voted for it, and no Republican voted against it. The stage was now set for a mammoth fight between Congress and the president.

THE BATTLE OVER RATIFICATION

Once Congress passed the Fourteenth Amendment, President Johnson couldn't stop it from being submitted to the states for ratification. He was so strongly opposed to it, however, that he took the unusual step of sending a message to Congress explaining his objections. Johnson claimed that Congress had no authority to pass a constitutional amendment as long as it unconstitutionally denied representation to the former Confederate states. Relying on its authority to determine the qualifications of its members, Congress still hadn't seated any southerners.

Like the Thirteenth Amendment, the Fourteenth Amendment needed the support of some of the former Confederate states to become part of the Constitution. Also, Congress evidently intended to make its ratification the price for the readmission of these states to full participation in the Union, although the amendment did not say so. Congress's intention became clear in July 1866, when it seated the members from Tennessee after that state ratified the Fourteenth Amendment.

By the end of February 1867, twenty states had ratified the amendment. However, two border states, Delaware and Kentucky, and the remaining ten former Confederate states had rejected it. At that point the Fourteenth Amendment's chances for adoption seemed to be poor. Congress therefore decided to force the issue. In one of its last acts, the Thirty-Ninth Congress imposed military rule on the South until its states ratified the Fourteenth Amendment. The Reconstruction Act, which was passed over the president's veto, also required these states to amend their constitutions to guarantee voting rights (or suffrage) to black men and forbade ex-Confederates disqualified from holding office under the proposed Fourteenth Amendment from taking part in the state constitutional conventions and from holding office in the new state governments. Faced with two undesirable alternatives, military rule or black voting rights, the South chose the former. With the president's encouragement the southern officials dragged their feet as long as possible in complying with the Reconstruction Act. Congress eventually passed three more Reconstruction Acts to force the South to comply with its terms for readmission.

The battle over ratification of the Fourteenth Amendment continued until July 9, 1868, when Louisiana and South Carolina ratified it, making it part of the Constitution. Arkansas, Florida, and North Carolina had ratified it earlier in the year. Alabama and Georgia ratified it a few days after it was adopted. Virginia ratified it in 1869, and Mississippi and Texas ratified it in 1870.

WHAT THE FOURTEENTH AMENDMENT DOES

Much of the Fourteenth Amendment is now obsolete. Section 2, relating to a reduction in the House membership of any state that denies or restricts the voting rights of its adult male citizens, was never enforced by Congress. This section has been superseded by later constitutional amendments. The third and fourth sections, relating to the disqualification of certain Confederates from holding office and to the Confederate and Union Civil War debts, no longer have any practical meaning. The first and fifth sections of this amendment still have major importance, however.

The first section of the Fourteenth Amendment is its most significant provision. The first sentence was designed to counteract the *Dred Scott* decision by specifically affirming that black Americans are citizens. The rest of the section forbids the states from abridging the privileges and immunities of citizens (a provision similar to that in Article IV, Section 2 of the Constitution), from depriving any person of life, liberty, or property without due process of law (a restatement of the Fifth Amendment's due-process clause), and from denying to any person within their jurisdiction the equal protection of the laws. This section is ambiguous, however. It doesn't state what is meant by privileges and immunities, due process, or equal protection, thus giving rise to a number of court decisions dealing with the meaning of these terms.

THE FOURTEENTH AMENDMENT AND CORPORATIONS

Although the Fourteenth Amendment was clearly designed to protect the rights of black Americans, its due-process clause was initially used to protect the property rights of corporations against state actions. In the early twentieth century the Supreme Court, recognizing that corporations are considered "persons" under the law, struck down a number of state laws regulating corporations on the ground that they violated the rights of the corporations to due process. By the middle of the century, however, the Court had shifted to a view that such regulations are generally within a state's power.

THE FOURTEENTH AMENDMENT AND INDIVIDUAL RIGHTS

At first the Supreme Court narrowly interpreted the Fourteenth Amendment's applicability to the rights of individuals. In 1873 the Court dealt with a claim by a group of white butchers that the state of Louisiana had violated their Fourteenth Amendment rights by giving a corporation exclusive rights to slaughter livestock in New Orleans, thereby driving all other butchering firms out of business. In *Slaughter-House Cases* the Court held that the amendment's privileges and immunities clause protects only those rights that are derived from the Constitution and federal law. The Court defined these rights narrowly, citing as examples the right of access to ports and navigable waterways, the right to run for federal office, to travel to the seat of government, and to be protected while on the high seas or in other countries. Although the Court acknowledged that the Fourteenth Amendment had been adopted primarily to protect the rights of black Americans, its narrow interpretation of the amendment's privileges and immunities clause severely restricted their ability to use this clause in asking the federal courts to step in when a state violated their rights.

In 1883 in *Civil Rights Cases* (a group of cases that the Court combined in one hearing) the Court held that an 1875 civil-rights law forbidding racial discrimination in inns, public transportation, and public places of amusement was unconstitutional because the Fourteenth Amendment applied only to the actions of states, not individuals.

In the twentieth century the Supreme Court, relying on the Fourteenth Amendment's guarantees of due process and equal protection of the law, has gradually expanded the amendment's scope regarding individual rights. The amendment is now generally interpreted as forbidding the states as well as the federal government from infringing on the protections spelled out in the Bill of Rights.

Black Americans were the first to benefit from the revised interpretation. Beginning in 1938 the Court struck down many state laws that discriminated against blacks in admission to schools and colleges, opportunities for employment, and other areas. One of the most significant Supreme Court rulings was its 1954 decision in *Brown* v. *Board of Education*. In that case the Court held in a unanimous ruling that racial segregation in public schools (a requirement that blacks and whites attend separate schools) violates the Fourteenth Amendment's equal-protection clause. The *Brown* decision, which radically transformed the nation's public schools, reversed an 1896 decision (*Plessy* v. *Ferguson*) that upheld racially segregated public facilities as long as they were substantially equal. In the *Brown* decision the Court said that segregated schools are inherently unequal.

Beginning in the early 1970s the Court has also applied the Fourteenth Amendment's equal-protection clause to the rights of women. A major decision regarding women was issued in June 1996. At that time the Supreme Court held that the Virginia Military Institute, a state-supported school, must admit qualified women. The opinion, written by Justice Ruth Bader Ginsburg, capped her quarter-century struggle on behalf of women's rights. Justice Ginsburg said that the school's policy of admitting only male students violated the equal-protection clause of the Fourteenth Amendment. While recognizing the school's long tradition of educating future male leaders, she said that however much that tradition serves the state's sons, it does nothing for its daughters. That, she added, is not equal protection.

THE FOURTEENTH AMENDMENT AND THE FEDERAL GOVERNMENT'S POWER

The Fourteenth Amendment has clearly enlarged the powers of the federal government, especially its judiciary branch. Federal courts today are often involved in matters such as public education and legislative apportionment that were once considered to be under the states' control. Not everyone accepts this expansion of the federal government's power without question. Some legal scholars argue that the Supreme Court decisions expanding the effect of the Fourteenth Amendment are unauthorized attempts to add new constitutional amendments without going through Congress and the states. Others believe, however, that most, if not all, of these decisions are mandated by the plain language of the Fourteenth Amendment.

VOTING RIGHTS FOR BLACK AMERICANS

THE FIFTEENTH AMENDMENT (1870)

SECTION 1. The right of citizens of the United States to vote shall not be denied or abridged by the United States or by any State on account of race, color, or previous condition of servitude.

SECTION 2. The Congress shall have power to enforce this article by appropriate legislation.

The issue of who controlled election procedures was controversial during both the 1787 constitutional convention and the ratification period. Some people wanted the states to have complete control over all elections, while others wanted Congress to be able to pass laws regarding national elections. Article I, Section 4 of the Constitution, which gives the states the authority to set the time, place, and manner of congressional elections but allows Congress to change these rules, was a compromise between the two opposing views. Six states that ratified the Constitution, not satisfied with this compromise, recommended amendments to limit Congress's power to regulate national elections. Congress did not follow these recommendations, however.

Article I, Section 2 also appears to give the states the power to set the qualifications for voting in both national and state elections. This section begins by stating: "The House of Representatives shall be composed of Members chosen every second Year by the People of the several States, and the Electors in each State shall have the qualifications requisite for Electors of the most numerous Branch of the State Legislature." In other words, to be eligible to vote for a member of the U.S. House of Representatives, a person must first be eligible to vote for a member of the state legislature. Thus, voting rights, which are fundamental to a democratic form of government, have traditionally been regarded as matters for the states to decide. Consequently, nationwide changes in voting rights have generally been accomplished by constitutional amendments instead of federal laws. The Constitution has been amended five times to allow new groups of Americans to vote or to make it easier for them to vote. The first of these five amendments, the Fifteenth, was adopted after the Civil War to protect the voting rights of black Americans in the South.

WHITE ATTEMPTS TO RESTRICT BLACK VOTING

In 1868, Congress voted to readmit seven additional southern states—Alabama, Arkansas, Florida, Georgia, Louisiana, North Carolina, and South Carolina—that had complied with the requirements of the Reconstruction Acts. (Tennessee had been readmitted in 1866, before these laws were passed.) As we have seen in the preceding chapter, one of the requirements of the Reconstruction Acts was the establishment of new state constitutions that provided voting rights for black men. The new black voters voted overwhelmingly Republican in the 1868 presidential election, helping the Republicans to win the electoral votes of seven of the eight southern states that had been readmitted up to that time.

Conservative white Democrats in the South realized that if they hoped to regain political power, they had to control or restrict black voting. They used two main tactics to accomplish this: intimidation and economic pressure. The Ku Klux Klan and similar white organizations carried out systematic acts of violence against both blacks and white Republicans to discourage them from voting. At the same time, whites applied economic pressure against blacks, such as threats to cut off their credit at white-owned stores, evict them from white-owned property, and fire them from their jobs to keep them from voting or force them to vote for Democratic candidates. (At that time elections were not held by secret ballot as they are today.)

CONGRESS PASSES
THE FIFTEENTH AMENDMENT

As reports of violence and intimidation in the South mounted, Republicans in Congress considered ways of providing more permanent protection of the voting rights of black southerners. The Republicans also wanted to preserve their own political power, since they knew that most blacks voted for Republicans. In February 1869, Congress passed a constitutional amendment forbidding the denial or abridgment of blacks' voting rights. Congress used these words because it didn't want to remove all authority over voting qualifications from the states. Ratification was completed in February 1870.

Despite Democratic opposition, the amendment had little trouble achieving ratification, even in the South. Most southern state governments were controlled by the Republicans at that time. The three southern states that had not yet been readmitted—Mississippi, Texas, and Virginia—also ratified the amendment quickly because of pressure to do so as part of the price for their readmission. These states were readmitted in 1870, after they ratified the amendment.

ENFORCEMENT OF THE FIFTEENTH AMENDMENT

Congress passed the first law enforcing the Fifteenth Amendment in May 1870. This law made those who tried to prevent qualified persons from voting subject to fines and imprisonment. In an effort to combat the actions of the Ku Klux Klan and other terrorist groups, the law also made it a federal crime to conspire with others to prevent citizens from voting or to harm those who exercised this right. In February 1871, Congress strengthened the 1870 law by placing congressional elections in cities with populations of over 20,000 under direct federal supervision. Finally, as reports of violence against black voters continued, Congress passed a third enforcement act in April 1871.

This law, called the Ku Klux Klan Act, declared that the actions of groups such as the Klan constituted a rebellion against the United States government, and gave the president the authority to impose martial law in the areas where violence and intimidation were widespread. (Under martial law, military instead of civilian officials enforce the law.) This provision was controversial. While it was being considered, most Democrats and even a few prominent Republicans opposed it because they felt that it gave the federal government too much power. (At that time the Democratic party generally believed in states' rights and a limited national government, while the Republican party defended broad powers for the federal government—the reverse of their political positions today.)

Federal troops were used to enforce the Fifteenth Amendment in several areas of the South in which violence was especially widespread. Hundreds of criminal charges were brought against Klan members accused of violence against blacks, and a few of the worst offenders were convicted and sentenced to prison. Many others went unpunished, however, because witnesses either agreed with their actions or were afraid to testify against them.

THE SUPREME COURT RULES
ON THE ENFORCEMENT ACTS

In 1876 the Supreme Court issued two decisions that effectively ended the federal government's ability to protect the voting rights of black Americans in the South, seeming to undermine the Fifteenth Amendment. One case, *U.S. v. Cruikshank*, involved three men who took part in a racially motivated riot in Louisiana. Under the provisions of the Enforcement Act of 1870, the men had been convicted of conspiracy to violate the civil rights of blacks. The Court not only overturned the convictions because of deficiencies in the wording of the charges but also declared that the Fifteenth Amendment gave the federal government authority only over state actions that violated the rights of blacks. The power to punish individuals who violated these rights still rested with the states, where it had always rested.

The other decision, in the case of *U.S. v. Reese*, involved an official who refused to accept and count a black man's vote in a local election. In this decision the Court held that two important sections of the 1870 law were unconstitutional because they were too broad in scope. The Court stated that the federal government's Fifteenth Amendment authority over the denial of voting rights applies only where the denial is based spe-

Although the Fifteenth Amendment said that the right to vote could not be denied anyone because of their race, the reality of blacks trying to vote in the South was not as simple. This cartoon seems to say that even if the law could no longer keep a black man away from the polls, violence and coercion still could.

cifically on race. The 1870 law as written did not confine itself to this narrow area.

The restrictive wording of the Fifteenth Amendment and these two decisions left the door open to state action that restricted black voting rights by setting up voting qualifications that blacks (but not whites) had difficulty meeting. As the Democrats gradually regained political power in the South, they passed a rash of discriminatory laws that kept most blacks from voting. In 1894 a Democratic Congress repealed most of the provisions for enforcing the Fifteenth Amendment.

GRANDFATHER CLAUSES

Many states had laws requiring that voters be able to read and write. These laws disqualified many uneducated persons, both black and white, from voting. After the end of the Reconstruction period, several southern states passed laws removing the need for a literacy test for the descendants of persons who could vote as of a specified date—one that occurred during a time in which blacks were barred from voting. Descendants of persons who were living in a foreign country on the specified date were also allowed to vote without taking a literacy test. These so-called Grandfather Clauses allowed the states to deny voting rights to uneducated blacks while granting them to whites.

In 1913 the Supreme Court heard arguments in two cases involving Grandfather Clauses in Oklahoma and Maryland. The lawyers who defended the Maryland law argued that Maryland, which had not ratified the Fifteenth Amendment, was not bound by it. They argued that the amendment itself was unconstitutional. In their opinion the right to determine for itself who should be allowed to vote in state and local elections was essential to a state's existence, and any restriction of that right was beyond the reach of the Constitution. The Court ignored this argument. In June 1915 it ruled that both the Maryland and Oklahoma laws were unconstitutional violations of the Fifteenth Amendment.

WHITE PRIMARIES

In the early part of the twentieth century most white southerners were Democrats. The Democrats dominated southern politics so thoroughly that the former Confederacy was called the Solid South. During that period blacks in some southern states were not allowed to vote in the primary elections, in which voters chose their party's candidates for public office. Although the primary in effect was the regular election in these one-party states, the Supreme Court initially held that voting qualifications for primary elections were political matters over which it had no jurisdiction. In 1944, however, the Court reversed itself, holding that the so-called white primaries violated the Fifteenth Amendment.

POLL TAXES

Another common obstacle to black voting was the poll tax. A number of states required the payment of a tax as a qualification for voting. Although these taxes were generally small, opponents argued that they prevented blacks, who often couldn't afford to pay them, from voting. The elimination of poll taxes is discussed in Chapter 12.

LITERACY TESTS

The most common device for restricting black voting in the South was the literacy test. In many parts of the South these tests were administered unfairly. While whites usually had to read only a few simple sentences to prove that they were literate, blacks often had to read and interpret complex provisions of state laws or constitutions before they were allowed to register to vote. In 1965, thanks to the efforts of both black and white civil-rights crusaders, Congress passed a law that removed this last barrier from the ability of southern blacks to vote on an equal basis with whites.

THE VOTING RIGHTS ACT OF 1965

This law, which would be in effect for five years, suspended literacy tests in areas where less than half of the voting age population had registered to vote, and authorized the U.S. attorney general to have federal registrars process voting registrations in areas that persisted in discriminatory voting practices, whether or not they employed literacy tests. Although the law affected a few areas outside the South, it primarily affected six southern states—Alabama, Georgia, Louisiana, Mississippi, South Carolina, and Virginia—and part of North Carolina.

The Supreme Court Upholds
the Voting Rights Act

In 1966 the Court upheld the Voting Rights Act as a valid enforcement of the Fifteenth Amendment. Eight justices joined in the decision, and a ninth, Justice Hugo L. Black, objected only to a part of the law that required states that were affected by it to obtain the approval of the U.S. attorney general for any changes in their election laws. Justice Black considered this provision an unconstitutional federal veto power over state laws.

Throughout the Civil War the prominent black spokesman Frederick Douglass had pressed for the achievement of three goals—the abolition of slavery, equality before the law, and voting rights—to complete the adoption of blacks into what he described as "the great national family of America." The adoption of the Thirteenth, Fourteenth, and Fifteenth Amendments accomplished Douglass's legal and political goals. Today black Americans in all sections of the country vote, hold public office, attend schools, hold jobs, and live in neighborhoods that once were barred to blacks. Whether they have been completely adopted into the American family is another matter, however. Many black Americans, particularly in large cities, still suffer from poverty and other social ills. The question of what to do about these problems still divides us. It seems unlikely that another constitutional amendment will help to solve the problems. Perhaps Douglass was right when he said, "Verily, the work does not end with the abolition of slavery, but only begins."[4]

TWO EARLY TWENTIETH-CENTURY AMENDMENTS

THE SIXTEENTH AMENDMENT (1913)
The Congress shall have power to lay and collect taxes on incomes, from whatever source derived, without apportionment among the several States, and without regard to any census or enumeration.

THE SEVENTEENTH AMENDMENT (1913)
The Senate of the United States shall be composed of two Senators from each state, elected by the people thereof, for six years; and each Senator shall have one vote. The electors in each State shall have the qualifications requisite for electors of the most numerous branch of the State legislatures.

When vacancies happen in the representation of any State in the Senate, the executive authority of such State shall issue writs of election to fill such vacancies: *Provided,* That the legislature of any State may empower the executive thereof to make temporary appointments until the people fill the vacancies by election as the legislature may direct.

This amendment shall not be so construed as to affect the election or term of any Senator chosen before it becomes valid as part of the Constitution.

After the adoption of three major constitutional amendments resulting from the Civil War and Reconstruction, more than forty years passed before the Constitution was amended again. In 1913 two related amendments were adopted. These amendments resulted in a major change in the federal tax structure and a change in the way U.S. senators are elected.

THE CONSTITUTION AND TAXES

Article I, Section 8, Clause 1 of the Constitution requires that all duties, imposts (taxes on imported goods), and excise taxes be uniform throughout the United States. Article I, Section 9, Clause 4 requires that direct taxes must be apportioned among the states according to their population. This provision of apportionment based on population was added at the insistence of delegates from southern states, who were afraid that a tax based on the number of acres of land a person held would result in high taxes for large landowners in the South, while landholders in the heavily populated areas of the North would pay less in taxes even though their smaller parcels of land might be more valuable than the southern land.

The apportionment (or setting a proportionate share) of taxes according to a state's population would be difficult if not impossible to accomplish. For example, a direct tax raised from a state with 10 percent of the country's total population would be limited to 10 percent of the total tax received from the entire country. Figuring the amount of the proportional tax would not only be difficult but could result in an uneven tax burden on individuals, depending on the state in which they lived.

Furthermore, Article I, Section 9, Clause 4 was made even more troublesome by the fact that the framers of the Constitution did not define the term "direct taxes." At one point delegate Rufus King of Massachusetts asked what this term meant. He did not receive an answer, possibly because the other delegates thought that Congress could raise enough money to pay its bills through duties on imports and excise taxes on goods such as liquor without resorting to these direct taxes, and that the point was probably moot (or debatable). One delegate, Gouverneur Morris of Pennsylvania, suggested that the entire clause regarding direct taxes be deleted. Unfortunately, this confusing provision remained to become a source of trouble that would eventually be eliminated by a constitutional amendment.

Hylton *v.* United States

In one of its earliest decisions the Supreme Court dealt with the issue of what is a direct tax. After Congress imposed a tax on individuals based on their ownership of carriages, one owner sued the government, claiming that the carriage tax was a direct tax that must be apportioned among the states according to their population. In 1796 the Supreme Court ruled in the case of *Hylton* v. *United States* that the carriage tax was not a direct tax. In the Court's opinion the Constitution considered only two types of taxes as direct taxes requiring apportionment: capitation (or poll) taxes, and taxes on land.

CORRUPT LAWMAKERS AND HIGH TARIFFS

Toward the end of the nineteenth century, Congress passed several laws imposing high tariffs on imported goods to protect American corporations from competition by foreign businesses. Many people didn't like these tariffs, which resulted in higher prices for the imported goods. They suspected that the large corporations controlled the votes of members of Congress, particularly senators, on the tariffs. Since the state legislatures elected U.S. senators, some people blamed these bodies for choosing men who could be relied on to do whatever the big corporations wanted them to do. As the nineteenth century neared an end, many Americans believed that the way to end high protective tariffs was to remove the election of senators from the state legislatures and place it in the hands of the people themselves.

There was one big problem in lowering tariffs, however. Import duties represented a large portion of the federal government's revenue. If Congress lowered tariffs, where could it find the money to pay the government's bills? The answer was a tax that affects almost all Americans today—the income tax.

INCOME TAXES

In 1894 southern and western Democrats succeeded in enacting a modest income tax by attaching it to a tariff bill. The law provided for a tax of 2 percent on all kinds of income over $4,000. Its supporters expected no argument regarding the tax's constitutionality. After all, in 1881 the Supreme Court had unanimously upheld an income tax that had been imposed during the Civil War but later repealed. One taxpayer, who was supported by wealthy and prominent opponents of income taxes, decided to challenge the new law anyway. One of his arguments was that income taxes were direct taxes which had to be apportioned among the states.

Pollock *v.* Farmers' Loan and Trust
The Supreme Court held two hearings in the case of *Pollock* v. *Farmers' Loan and Trust,* which challenged the constitutionality of the 1894 income tax law. After

the first hearing, the Court ruled that taxes on the income from land were direct taxes, but split evenly on the issue of the constitutionality of some of the other parts of the law. After the second hearing, the Court ruled in 1895 by a five-to-four majority that the entire income tax law was unconstitutional. Although the Court acknowledged that it would be impossible to apportion taxes based on personal property or income among the states, it nevertheless concluded that they were direct taxes. The Court added that a constitutional amendment would be required before the federal government could tax any kind of personal property or the income received from such property.

The *Pollock* decision, which reversed two previous Supreme Court decisions, one of which had been made only fourteen years earlier, was both unexpected and controversial. Charles Evans Hughes, who served on the Supreme Court as an associate justice from 1910 to 1916 and as chief justice from 1930 to 1941, often referred to this decision in later years as one of the court's worst "self-inflicted wounds," which seriously damaged its authority. (Hughes put the 1857 *Dred Scott* decision in the same category.)[5]

CONGRESS PASSES THE
SIXTEENTH AMENDMENT

Despite the unpopularity of the *Pollock* decision, it took fourteen years for Congress to pass a constitutional amendment to authorize the federal government to impose income taxes without apportioning them among the states. The main reason for the delay was a widespread belief that such an amendment, which would greatly increase the power of the federal government, stood little or no chance for ratification by the states. On July 12, 1909, following President William Howard

Taft's recommendation, Congress passed the Sixteenth Amendment, still expecting the states to reject it. Congress was wrong. The states gradually ratified the amendment during the next four years. Only a handful of states rejected it outright. On February 5, 1913, New Mexico, which had been admitted as a state the previous year, became the thirty-sixth of the forty-eight states to ratify the amendment, making it part of the Constitution.

Today the income tax, which is the main source of revenue for the federal government, is still extremely controversial. Some people still call for the elimination of income taxes and a corresponding reduction in the spending of the federal government to offset the deficit that would result from the reduction in revenue. Congress has not seriously considered repealing the Sixteenth Amendment, however.

DIRECT ELECTION OF U.S. SENATORS

While the ratification of the Constitution was being considered, some Anti-Federalists complained about the excessive power of the Senate. They also pointed out that senators, not being elected by the people, wouldn't be accountable to them. These objections were overruled, but some Americans continued to believe that senators should be elected by the people instead of the state legislatures.

POPULISTS AND PROGRESSIVES

Congress didn't pay much attention to demands for the popular election of U.S. senators until near the end of the nineteenth century, when a new political party was formed. The People's (or Populist) party, which was formed in 1892, called for several reforms. Among these were lower tariffs and the direct election of senators.

The party, which attracted members mainly in the South and West, didn't last long. By the turn of the century it had been almost completely absorbed into the Democratic party. The Populists were influential, however, in getting the House of Representatives to consider a constitutional amendment requiring the direct election of U.S. senators. Beginning in 1893 the House passed such an amendment repeatedly, only to have the proposal fail to gain Senate approval. This wasn't surprising. By approving a change in the way they were elected, the senators risked being defeated in future elections.

The tide was turning, however. In the early years of the twentieth century, a group of reformers called Progressives campaigned for various changes in government. Continuing reports of widespread political corruption in the state legislatures as well as the desire for a more democratic government motivated these reformers to call for a greater popular voice in the selection of U.S. senators. In response to the demands of the Progressives some states began to hold primary elections in which the voters chose candidates for the Senate. The state legislators then voted for the winners of the primaries. By 1912, twenty-nine states used this method of choosing candidates for the U.S. Senate.

CONGRESS PASSES THE SEVENTEENTH AMENDMENT

The advocates of the popular election of senators received their final boost in 1911, when a senator from Illinois was found to have been fraudulently elected by the legislature. The uproar over the fraudulent election couldn't be ignored. On May 13, 1912, Congress passed the Seventeenth Amendment. Ratification took less than a year to complete. The amendment became part of the Constitution on April 8, 1913.

The Seventeenth Amendment undoubtedly made the election of U.S. senators a more democratic process. However, it is questionable whether the direct election of senators has reduced the amount of corruption in government. Scandals, many of them involving attempts by large corporations to influence public policy, still turn up from time to time. Those scandals implicate both federal and state officials. Maybe they are the inevitable result of the power that comes with holding a public office. Nevertheless, most Americans want public officials to maintain high ethical standards.

Within ten years after the adoption of the Sixteenth and Seventeenth Amendments, two more constitutional amendments were added in response to campaigns by Progressive reformers. The adoption of the Eighteenth (or Prohibition) Amendment is regarded as a failure today—a failure so complete that it led to the adoption of another constitutional amendment (the Twenty-First Amendment) to repeal it less than fifteen years after it was added to the Constitution. The other reform, the adoption of the Nineteenth Amendment to grant voting rights to American women, was successful.

VOTING RIGHTS FOR WOMEN

Some constitutional amendments have been adopted
quickly, while others have resulted from concerted efforts over many years. The drive for voting rights for
women, like the crusade to abolish slavery and the push
for a nationwide ban on the manufacture and sale of
alcoholic beverages, took many years to accomplish its
goal. Almost three-quarters of a century elapsed from the
time that a small group set out to obtain legal and political rights for American women until the adoption of the
Nineteenth Amendment in 1920.

ABOLITION AND WOMEN'S RIGHTS

The drive for the abolition of slavery was supported by
women as well as men. As women learned more about
the plight of the slaves, some of them began to draw

comparisons between slavery and their own situation. In the mid-nineteenth century American women had few legal or political rights. Moreover, their choices regarding education and work were limited. They couldn't vote or hold public office. Most colleges didn't admit women students. Married women generally couldn't own property in their own names or control their own money. Few occupations were open to women workers. Besides, it wasn't considered respectable for a married woman to work outside her own home if her husband was able to support the family. Most people, women as well as men, accepted this state of affairs, believing that women's primary role was the care of their homes and families. Politics and other outside activities were best left to men.

THE SENECA FALLS CONVENTION

In 1848 five women in upstate New York decided to call a convention to discuss ways of obtaining more rights for American women. Only one, Lucretia Mott, had any previous experience in organizing a meeting or in public speaking. (Mott had organized the Philadelphia Female Anti-Slavery Society in 1833.) The women didn't let that stand in their way, however. The two-day meeting, which attracted more than a hundred men and women, took place on July 19 and 20, 1848, in Seneca Falls, New York. During the meeting two of the women, Mott and Elizabeth Cady Stanton, presented a statement entitled "A Declaration of Rights and Sentiments."

The two women had different ideas about women's rights. Mott believed that the most important goal was economic rights for women, while Stanton believed that the right to vote was essential to every other reform. Despite Mott's concern that advocating voting rights for women was too radical an idea, Stanton included a call for such rights in the declaration. After Frederick Douglass spoke at the meeting in support of women's right to vote, the group endorsed it in a close vote.

The Seneca Falls declaration was not generally well received. Most newspaper editors and church leaders either condemned it or ridiculed it. Despite the adverse reaction, the people who signed the statement at Seneca Falls persisted in their efforts. In 1850 a women's rights convention in Worcester, Massachusetts, was attended by more than a thousand people. Afterward, women's rights conventions were held every year until the start of the Civil War.

WOMEN AND THE CIVIL WAR AMENDMENTS

During the Civil War the advocates of women's rights put aside their own concerns temporarily. As the war drew to a close, many of them joined in the campaign for the adoption of the Thirteenth Amendment. They divided, however, on the question of supporting the Fourteenth and Fifteenth Amendments. After an unsuccessful attempt to get the word "male" removed from the wording of Section 2 of the Fourteenth Amendment (see Chapter 6), Stanton and her fellow advocate of women's rights Susan B. Anthony opposed the adoption of the Fourteenth and Fifteenth Amendments because they gave rights to black men that were denied to women. However, most reformers at that time, including large numbers of women, disagreed with Anthony and Stanton. They didn't want to risk defeat by including too many controversial issues in these amendments. They also thought that blacks, who had suffered greater injustices, were more in need of protection than women.

TWO RIVAL WOMAN
SUFFRAGE ORGANIZATIONS

In May 1869, Anthony, Stanton, and a few friends formed the National Woman Suffrage Association to campaign for voting rights for women. Because of Anthony's and Stanton's opposition to the Fourteenth and Fifteenth Amendments, many women who wanted to work for woman suffrage believed they were too radical and refused to join their organization. In November 1869 a group of more conservative women under the leadership of Lucy Stone organized the American Woman Suffrage Association.

In 1872, Anthony tested the idea that the Fourteenth Amendment's declaration that all persons born in the United States and subject to its jurisdiction were American citizens gave women the right to vote. Ignoring her earlier opposition to the amendment, Anthony voted in that year's presidential election. She was later convicted in a federal court of unlawful voting and fined one hundred dollars. In another case involving a woman's attempt to vote, the Supreme Court ruled in 1874 that citizenship does not in itself provide voting rights.

The National Woman Suffrage Association organized a drive for a constitutional amendment giving women the same voting rights as men. Although sympathetic members of Congress introduced resolutions proposing the amendment (which became known as the Susan B. Anthony amendment) and congressional committees held hearings on the proposals, nothing much came of it. The American Woman Suffrage Association, on the other hand, tried to get the individual states to grant voting rights to women instead of pushing for a national constitutional amendment. Eventually it became obvious that the rivalry was hurting the women suffrage cause, and in 1890 the two organizations merged, taking the name National American Woman Suffrage Association. Stanton was named president of the new organization, with Anthony as her vice president and Stone as head of the executive committee. In 1892, Anthony succeeded Stanton as president of the association.

THE CAMPAIGN FOR WOMAN SUFFRAGE IN THE STATES

Shortly after Anthony became president, the woman suffrage organization abandoned its drive for a constitutional amendment and went back to Stone's idea of getting the individual states to allow women to vote. This strategy had some success, especially in the western states. By the end of 1912 nine states allowed women to vote, but in that year three heavily populated states (Michigan, Ohio, and Wisconsin) defeated woman suffrage proposals. Some of the suffragists, frustrated by the slow pace of reform, favored a bolder approach.

The Congressional Union and the Woman's Party

In March 1913 these women organized a parade in Washington, D.C., to press for a woman suffrage amendment. The group was headed by Alice Paul, a social worker who had worked for the woman suffrage movement in England. Although they had permission for the march, the five thousand women endured insults, shoving, and jostling at the hands of a hostile mob while the city police force did little or nothing to help them. It took a group of army cavalry troops to restore order and allow the women to finish their march. The episode produced a nationwide surge of sympathy for the women. Petitions for a woman suf-

*The fight for woman suffrage involved many
dedicated people and many forceful debates over
many frustrating years. This woman picketing outside
the White House had just three years to wait until the
passage of the Nineteenth Amendment.*

frage amendment were gathered and presented to members of Congress, and delegations began to meet with the new president, Woodrow Wilson, to ask for his help.

In April 1913, Alice Paul formed the Congressional Union to work for a constitutional amendment. The leaders of the national suffrage organization were still not sure whether Paul's strategy was wise, however. In 1914, after it became clear that the two groups couldn't reconcile their differences, Paul and her supporters left the national association. Two years later, Paul formed a new political party, the Woman's party, to continue the drive for a constitutional amendment.

Meanwhile, the state-by-state approach ran into serious trouble. In 1914 seven states voted on woman suffrage. Only two sparsely populated states, Montana and Nevada, granted voting rights to women that year. In 1915 proposals for woman suffrage were defeated in four heavily populated eastern states (Massachusetts, New Jersey, New York, and Pennsylvania). After these defeats, the president of the national association resigned.

CARRIE CHAPMAN CATT'S WINNING PLAN

Things looked bleak for the national woman suffrage association. The 1915 defeats and the rivalry with the Congressional Union had demoralized many of its members. Besides, the organization was almost bankrupt. In desperation the association asked a former president, Carrie Chapman Catt, to head the group a second time. Catt's selection proved to be a turning point. A skilled organizer and forceful leader, Catt, who had recently received a substantial inheritance earmarked for the woman suffrage drive, also provided some much-needed money.

During 1916, which was a presidential election year, both of the rival woman suffrage groups tried to get the two major political parties to endorse voting rights for women. Both parties gave halfhearted support to woman suffrage. Afterward, the Woman's party engaged in a fruitless campaign against President Wilson (who was running for reelection) in the states that allowed women to vote. Catt, who realized that she couldn't afford to antagonize any political leaders, tried to stay on good terms with the president and the members of both parties in Congress. Meanwhile, Catt worked on what she called a "winning plan." Her organization would continue efforts to get more states to give women voting rights. At the same time they would try to get Congress to pass a constitutional amendment and they would begin planning a campaign for ratification in the few states where women already had voting rights.

The entry of the United States into World War I in 1917 complicated matters for Catt. After the war began in 1914, Catt and other women opponents of war (called pacifists) had formed the Woman's Peace party to work for world peace. When it seemed certain that the United States would enter the war, Catt convinced the national suffrage association that opposition to the war would not only be useless but would also hurt its cause. Instead of engaging in protests against the war, as the Woman's party did, Catt's groups supported the war effort. It also continued its campaign for woman suffrage. The combination of the two activities—helping the war effort and pushing for voting rights—had some success. By the end of 1917 several states had given women the right to vote in presidential elections. Others allowed women to vote for school boards or in other local elections. Moreover, the women won the biggest prize of all when New York gave women voting rights in 1917.

CONGRESS PASSES THE
NINETEENTH AMENDMENT

In January 1918, while the House of Representatives prepared to vote on the Susan B. Anthony amendment, President Wilson announced his support of it. The amendment passed the House on January 10, 1918, by the exact number needed for a two-thirds majority. However, the Senate delayed its vote until late September. Shortly before the Senate voted, the president took the unusual step of addressing its members in person to urge the passage of the amendment. Despite his plea, the Senate failed by two votes to give it the necessary two-thirds majority. When the Senate voted on the amendment again in February 1919, it failed by one vote.

In May 1919, President Wilson called the incoming Congress into special session to consider the peace proposals that he and America's allies had drafted. He also used this opportunity to again urge passage of the Anthony amendment. This time both the Senate and the House responded to his urgings. On June 4, 1919, Congress passed the Nineteenth Amendment.

THE BATTLE OVER RATIFICATION

The opponents of woman suffrage, who were well organized, fought hard to stop the ratification of the amendment. Some state governors who opposed it refused to call their state legislatures into session to vote on it. In other states the opponents of the amendment insisted that it had to be submitted to the voters in a referendum even though the legislature had already ratified it. In June 1920 the Supreme Court ruled that state referenda on constitutional amendments were not required for a state's ratification. Finally, on August 18,

1920, Tennessee became the thirty-sixth state to ratify the Nineteenth Amendment, making it part of the Constitution in time to allow women in every state to vote in that year's presidential election. Many of those who opposed the Nineteenth Amendment were afraid that women voters would endorse idealistic reforms that could open the door to socialism and even communism. Some also feared that women would eventually dominate American politics. The expected revolution didn't happen, however. Today, more than three-quarters of a century after women obtained the right to vote, women, who make up slightly over half the nation's population, are still a small minority in Congress. Things are gradually changing, however. By 1998, there were nine women in the U.S. Senate, more than fifty women in the House of Representatives, and two women on the Supreme Court. Two women governors and countless other women held offices in state and local governments. And women's votes are regarded as an important factor in national elections.

PROHIBITION
AND REPEAL

THE EIGHTEENTH AMENDMENT (1919)
SECTION 1. After one year from the ratification of this article the manufacture, sale, or transportation of intoxicating liquors within, the importation thereof into, or the exportation thereof from the United States and all territory subject to the jurisdiction thereof for beverage purposes is hereby prohibited.

SECTION 2. The Congress and the several States shall have concurrent power to enforce this article by appropriate legislation.

SECTION 3. This article shall be inoperative unless it shall have been ratified as an amendment to the Constitution by the legislatures of the several States, as provided in the Constitution, within seven years from the date of the submission hereof to the States by the Congress.

THE TWENTY-FIRST AMENDMENT (1933)
SECTION 1. The eighteenth article of amendment to the Constitution of the United States is hereby repealed.

SECTION 2. The transportation or importation into any State, Territory, or possession of the United States for delivery or use therein of intoxicating liquors, in violation of the laws thereof, is hereby prohibited.

SECTION 3. This article shall be inoperative unless it shall have been ratified as an amendment to the Constitution by conventions in the several States, as provided in the Constitution, within seven years from the date of the submission hereof to the States by the Congress.

The Eighteenth Amendment, which prohibited the manufacture and sale of alcoholic beverages throughout the United States, was added to the Constitution in January 1919, less than five months before Congress passed the Nineteenth Amendment, giving American women the right to vote on equal terms with men. The two amendments were related. Both resulted from repeated attempts over many years to achieve desired reforms. Both were affected by the entry of the United States into World War I. Moreover, the same groups tended to support both amendments.

THE TEMPERANCE MOVEMENT

Many Americans, especially those who belonged to conservative Protestant churches, advocated the practice of temperance (limiting the use of alcohol or abstaining altogether from its use) to avoid the problems associated with excessive drinking. By the middle of the nineteenth century some of them, convinced that drinking itself was sinful, began to call for a ban on the sale of alcoholic beverages. In 1851 the state of Maine prohibited the sale of liquor throughout the state (a ban that remained in effect until 1933). By the time the Civil War began, twelve other states had passed prohibition laws, and many local governments also banned or restricted the sale of alcoholic beverages.

After the end of the Civil War, most of these laws were either repealed by the state and local governments or overturned by the courts. The easy access to alcohol increased the problems related to excessive drinking. Men who drank too much often spent their wages on liquor. They also were frequently absent from work or under the influence of alcohol when they did show up at the workplace, resulting in the loss of their jobs. Their excessive drinking often left their wives and children dependent on relatives, friends, or local charities for food, clothing, and shelter. Some of these men even beat their wives and children.

These problems were especially noticeable in the cities, where saloons seemed to spring up on every street corner. The cities also contained large numbers of immigrants from countries such as Ireland and Germany, where the use of alcohol was more socially acceptable. These newcomers regarded the neighborhood saloon as a gathering place, where they could relax after a day's work and enjoy the company of their friends while having a few drinks. Most of the immigrants did not drink excessively, but the temperance advocates tended to blame them for the social ills associated with too much drinking. A mixture of nativism (anti-immigrant bias) and concern over the real problems caused by alcohol led to a push for its prohibition.

In 1869 a group of prohibition advocates formed the Prohibition party, which favored a nationwide ban on the sale of liquor. The party never became a major factor in national elections, but it played an important part, together with other temperance groups, in a continuing drive for nationwide prohibition.

THE WOMAN'S CHRISTIAN TEMPERANCE UNION

In 1874 a group of women reformers organized the Woman's Christian Temperance Union to combat the growing liquor trade. Under the leadership of Frances Willard, a former college professor who served as its president from 1879 until her death in 1898, the organization thrived, increasing its membership and spreading into many parts of the country. Willard, who served on the Prohibition party's executive committee from 1882 to 1891, persuaded the party to endorse voting rights for women as a means for achieving a ban on liquor. Willard reasoned that women, who were apt to suffer the most from the effects of excessive drinking by male family members, would tend to vote for Prohibition candidates.

THE ANTI-SALOON LEAGUE

The Anti-Saloon League, which started in Ohio in 1893, was a key element in the drive for nationwide prohibition. The national group, which was organized in 1895, set up a comprehensive program that trained leaders of state and local chapters in ways to recruit new members, raise money, and engage in political action. The League also started its own publishing company, which produced a monthly magazine, *The American Issue*, as well as pamphlets and other materials advocating temperance and denouncing the evils of drinking. Wayne Bidwell Wheeler, an Anti-Saloon League lawyer, drafted prohibition laws for national, state, and local governments and developed arguments for their supporters to use in getting these laws passed. He also worked for the election of prohibition candidates at all levels of government and the defeat of elected officials who did not support prohibition.

LAWS ON THE INTERSTATE
LIQUOR TRADE

In the late nineteenth century, advocates of prohibition were instrumental in getting several states to forbid the sale of liquor within the state. They couldn't eliminate the use of liquor, however, as long as it continued to be shipped in from other states. After the Supreme Court struck down an Iowa law that restricted the shipment of liquor into the state by interstate railroads, Congress passed a law in 1890 that subjected the railroads to the laws of the state to which liquor was shipped. The Supreme Court upheld this law in 1891. In 1913, Congress passed an even stricter law designed to stop the shipment of liquor to individuals in "dry states"—states with prohibition laws—for their personal use. (Advocates of prohibition were called drys, while those who opposed prohibition were called wets.) In 1917 the Supreme Court upheld the 1913 law, which had been passed over President William Howard Taft's veto.

THE CAMPAIGN FOR A PROHIBITION AMENDMENT

In December 1913 about 4,000 members of the Anti-Saloon League marched to the Capitol in Washington to ask Congress to pass a prohibition amendment. In 1914 a majority of the House of Representatives voted for the amendment, but it fell far short of the required two-thirds vote. The Anti-Saloon League then turned its attention to the next congressional election. The League's efforts were instrumental in electing a predominantly dry Congress in 1916.

WARTIME PROHIBITION LAWS

After the United States entered World War I, President Wilson asked for a number of laws designed to mobilize the American economy for an all-out war effort. In the summer of 1917 dry congressmen succeeded in amending a food-control bill to prohibit the use of grain for the manufacture of liquor on the grounds that such use reduced the amount of food available for the war effort. Supporters of prohibition also persuaded the War Department to ban the sale of liquor in the vicinity of military installations and to forbid members of the armed forces from buying drinks.

CONGRESS PASSES THE EIGHTEENTH AMENDMENT

One of the first acts of the incoming Congress in December 1917 was the passage of a constitutional amendment to forbid the manufacture, sale, or transportation of intoxicating liquor throughout the United States. The Eighteenth Amendment, which Congress passed on December 18, 1917, was adopted on January 16, 1919. The amendment gave both the states and the federal government the authority to enforce it. In October 1919, Congress passed the Volstead Act to enforce the Prohibition amendment, which took effect in January 1920.

The beer and liquor interests, faced with the loss of their businesses, challenged the validity of the Eighteenth Amendment. Two states, New Jersey and Rhode Island, also challenged it. (New Jersey ratified the amendment in 1922, but Rhode Island never ratified it.) The Supreme Court combined seven of these challenges and issued its decision upholding the validity of both the amendment and the Volstead Act on June 1, 1920.

THE RESULTS OF PROHIBITION

The supporters of Prohibition hoped to compel people to stop drinking alcohol by making alcoholic beverages unavailable. Instead, thriving new businesses sprang up as enterprising Americans set up illegal breweries and distilleries, smuggled alcohol into the country, and opened illegal drinking places. New words such as

With Prohibition, it was hoped that families
and society at large would be saved from the
ravages of alcohol. Instead, Prohibition created
a whole new set of problems, including the
widespread illegal manufacture and sale of
alcoholic beverages. Here, a man destroys barrels
of beer in the street as a small crowd looks on.

bootlegger (a person who carries illegal liquor in his boots) and speakeasy (a term derived from the practice of whispering a password to enter a place where liquor was served) became commonplace. Violent crime increased in the country's major cities as rival gangs fought for the control of the profitable traffic in illegal alcohol. Police forces and local government officials seemed either unable or unwilling to stop the criminal activities. Although Prohibition undoubtedly resulted in a decline in the consumption of alcoholic beverages, many Americans, particularly in the large cities, began to wonder about its wisdom.

THE CAMPAIGN FOR REPEAL OF PROHIBITION

In 1925 the Association Against the Prohibition Amendment was formed to work for the repeal of the Eighteenth Amendment. In 1928 a group of New York City lawyers formed the Voluntary Committee of Lawyers, which tried to persuade state and local lawyers' organizations, called bar associations, to endorse the repeal of Prohibition. The committee soon got the bar associations of several of the country's largest cities to endorse a repeal amendment.

In 1929 the newly elected president, Herbert Hoover, responded to the complaints about the enforcement of Prohibition by appointing an eleven-member commission to study the entire federal criminal justice system. The commission, which was headed by George W. Wickersham, a former attorney general during the Taft administration, consisted of prominent lawyers, judges, educators, and political leaders. After a comprehensive study that included such areas as juvenile crime, the prison system, and the court system, the committee issued fourteen separate reports. One report, issued in

January 1931, dealt with the enforcement of the country's Prohibition laws.

Although each of the eleven members of the Wickersham Commission drew separate conclusions regarding Prohibition, ten of them agreed that the Eighteenth Amendment should not be repealed. In submitting the commission's report on Prohibition to Congress, President Hoover stated that he agreed with the majority recommendation regarding this issue.

Opponents of Prohibition then published their own conclusions on the Wickersham Commission's report. Using the commission's own statements as the basis for their views, they argued that the Eighteenth Amendment was unenforceable because it did not have the support of law-abiding citizens, it did not bring about temperance, it tended to increase crime and corruption, and it damaged the administration of justice and created disrespect for law.

CONGRESS PASSES THE TWENTY-FIRST AMENDMENT

During the 1932 election campaign, the main issue facing both political parties was the deepening economic depression. However, the Republicans, whose ranks included many drys from rural areas and small towns, simply announced their willingness to submit a constitutional amendment to the states so that citizens could express their wishes regarding Prohibition. The Democrats, whose members included a large number of wets from urban areas, stated flatly that they favored the repeal of the Eighteenth Amendment. The election resulted in a Democratic president, Franklin Delano Roosevelt, and a Democratic Congress, which seemed certain to pass the repeal amendment when it met in December 1933. However, in the final days of its existence the outgoing Congress passed the Twenty-first Amendment, which called for the repeal of Prohibition. The amendment, which Congress passed on February 20, 1933, called for ratification by state conventions rather than the state legislatures to make it clear that a state's action on the amendment showed the will of the people. Also, the amendment's supporters were afraid that many state legislatures, which were controlled by drys, would vote against it. The amendment also included a seven-year time limit for ratification, a practice that had begun with the Eighteenth Amendment.

Nationwide Prohibition ended on December 5, 1933, after thirty-six of the forty-eight states ratified the Twenty-first Amendment. The states still had the authority to continue Prohibition within their own borders, but many of them quickly passed laws making the manufacture and sale of alcoholic beverages legal once again. By 1936 only eight states imposed prohibition on a statewide basis, and by 1966 all the states allowed the sale of liquor unless local laws prohibited it.

Shortly before Congress passed the Twenty-first Amendment to end Prohibition, another amendment was added to the Constitution. The Twentieth Amendment, which Congress passed on March 2, 1932, was adopted on January 23, 1933.

THREE AMENDMENTS
THAT AFFECT
THE PRESIDENCY

Twelve amendments were added to the Constitution in the twentieth century. Three of them, adopted within a thirty-five year period, affected the office of president of the United States. These amendments change the dates on which presidents take office, restrict them to two terms of office, and establish rules to deal with situations in which the president fails to complete his term or is unable to carry out the duties of his office.

THE TWENTIETH AMENDMENT (1933)

SECTION 1. The terms of the President and Vice President shall end at noon on the 20th day of January, and the terms of Senators and Representatives at noon on the 3d day of January, of the years in which such terms would have ended if this article had not been ratified; and the terms of their successors shall then begin.

SECTION 2. The Congress shall assemble at least once in every year, and such meeting shall begin at noon on the 3d day of January, unless they shall by law appoint a different day.

SECTION 3. If, at the time fixed for the beginning of the term of the President, the President elect shall have died, the Vice President elect shall become President. If a President shall not have been chosen before the time fixed for the beginning of his term, or if the President elect shall have failed to qualify, then the Vice President elect shall act as President until a President shall have qualified; and the Congress may by law provide for the case wherein neither a President elect nor a Vice President elect shall have qualified, declaring who shall then act as President, or the manner in which one who is to act shall be selected, and such person shall act accordingly until a President or Vice President shall have qualified.

SECTION 4. The Congress may by law provide for the case of the death of any of the persons from whom the House of Representatives may choose a President whenever the right of choice shall have devolved upon them, and for the case of the death of any of the persons from whom the Senate may choose a Vice President whenever the right of choice shall have devolved upon them.

SECTION 5. Sections 1 and 2 shall take effect on the 15th day of October following the ratification of this article.

SECTION 6. This article shall be inoperative unless it shall have been ratified as an amendment to the Constitution by the legislatures of three-fourths of the several States within seven years from the date of its submission.

After President Roosevelt took office on March 4, 1933, he immediately called the new Congress, which wasn't due to meet until December, into special session to consider ways of dealing with the deep economic depression that gripped the country. The federal officials who took office in 1933 were the last to operate under that timetable. On October 15, 1933, the Twentieth Amendment took effect, changing the dates on which the president and Congress begin their terms of office.

THE ORIGINAL RULES ON
TERMS OF OFFICE

It had been obvious for many years that something needed to be done about the dates on which new Congresses met. Article I, Section 4 of the Constitution provided that Congress was to meet at least once each year on the first Monday in December unless Congress passed a law appointing a different meeting date. The First Congress, which was elected in 1788, took office on March 4, 1789 (the date set by the outgoing Confederation Congress). Since the terms of members of the House of Representatives ran for two years (as did those of one-third of the first group of senators chosen under the new Constitution), the First Congress ended its existence in March 1791. Members of the Second Congress, who were elected in 1790, couldn't take office in December 1790 because the terms of their predecessors hadn't yet expired, so they had to wait until the following December to begin their terms. Members of subsequent Congresses also didn't take office until more than a year after being elected.

This arrangement made sense in the late eighteenth century, when travel to the nation's capital often involved traveling over rough roads that were little more than dirt tracks. As travel conditions improved, the interval between the election of new members of Congress and their assumption of office made less and less sense. Moreover, presidents often found it necessary to call a new Congress into session before the scheduled December meeting to deal with urgent matters.

LAME DUCKS

There was an additional problem with the existing time frame. Members of Congress who had lost a bid for reelection, called lame ducks, continued in office for several months. The sessions of Congress that followed an election were called lame-duck sessions. Defeated members of Congress sometimes voted for bills that were unpopular with the general public or voted against popular bills in the hope of winning jobs or other favors from powerful groups that agreed with their action.

THE LAME-DUCK AMENDMENT

Although there were many calls for changes in the dates on which the president and members of Congress took office, nothing much was done until the presidency of Warren G. Harding, who was elected in 1920. In the 1922 election the Republicans in Congress suffered heavy losses. During the lame-duck session following that election, many of these lame-duck congressmen, who hoped to win a political appointment from the president, voted for a bill that Harding had proposed to help American shipbuilders. Their votes on this so-called ship subsidy bill, which was very unpopular with the public and with other members of Congress, spurred Senator George Norris of Nebraska, a progressive Republican who had supported such reforms as the income tax amendment, direct election of senators, and voting rights for women, to introduce a constitutional amendment.

The Senate passed Norris's proposed amendment in February 1923, toward the end of that lame-duck session, but the House failed to consider it. The amendment was passed by the Senate three more times, but failed to win House approval. Finally, after the Democrats took control of the House in the 1930 elections, that body passed the amendment in March 1932. Ratification was completed on January 23, 1933.

The Twentieth Amendment changed the date on which members of Congress take office to January 3 of

(116)

the year following their election, significantly reducing the time lag between election and assumption of office and the tenure of lame-duck members. It also set a date for the president's assumption of office (something the Constitution didn't specify previously). The president's term of office begins on January 20 of the year following the presidential election, ensuring that Congress is in session when the president takes office. The amendment also sets procedures to be followed in case a newly elected president dies before taking office.

THE TWENTY-SECOND AMENDMENT (1951)

SECTION 1. No person shall be elected to the office of the President more than twice, and no person who has held the office of President, or acted as President, for more than two years of a term to which some other person was elected President shall be elected to the office of the President more than once. But this Article shall not apply to any person holding the office of President when this Article was proposed by the Congress, and shall not prevent any person who may be holding the office of President, or acting as President, during the term within which this Article becomes operative from holding the office of President or acting as President during the remainder of such term.

SECTION 2. This article shall be inoperative unless it shall have been ratified as an amendment to the Constitution by the legislatures of three-fourths of the several States within seven years from the date of its submission to the States by the Congress.

President Roosevelt, who was reelected by an overwhelming majority in 1936, began his second term on January 20, 1937, under the new rules created by the Twentieth Amendment. He took the oath of office as president twice more, in 1941 and 1945. His unprecedented reelection to a third and fourth term set off a reaction that eventually resulted in the adoption of the Twenty-second Amendment.

THE FUROR OVER A THIRD TERM

In 1936, when Roosevelt was elected to his second term, the country was still in a deep depression. By 1940 a new crisis, World War II, had arisen. Although many Americans wanted to stay out of the European war, it seemed increasingly likely that the United States would be drawn into the conflict. Moreover, relations between the United States and Japan were deteriorating. The growing threat of war convinced many Americans that the president should stay in office for another four years. However, that would break a precedent set more than 140 years earlier, when George Washington declined to accept a third term. Since that time no American president had served more than two terms.

Although Roosevelt refused to state his wishes regarding a third term, in July 1940 the Democratic National Convention nominated him by an overwhelming majority. Republicans (and some Democrats) then began warning that the president might try to establish himself as a dictator. Some people began to talk about term limits for American presidents, and in September and October a congressional subcommittee held hearings on this issue.

The idea of term limits for the president wasn't new. The 1787 constitutional convention considered a proposal to have the president serve a single six-year term. The proposal was defeated after its opponents pointed out that the possibility of being reelected might keep a president on his best behavior, whereas a person who knew he could hold office for only one term would have little incentive to do a good job.

Despite the talk about term limits, Roosevelt was elected to a third term in 1940. In 1944 the United States was at war, following Japan's attack on the American naval base at Pearl Harbor, Hawaii, on December 7, 1941. Although prospects for an American victory were good in 1944, many Americans believed that it would be unwise to change the country's political leadership in the midst of war. In November 1944, Roosevelt was elected to a fourth term. In April 1945, Roosevelt died in office and his vice president, Harry S. Truman, became president.

CONGRESS PASSES THE
TWENTY-SECOND AMENDMENT

In the 1946 national elections (the first since the end of World War II in August 1945) the Republicans, who had been out of power for fourteen years, gained control of Congress. The Republican Congress promptly introduced resolutions for a constitutional amendment limiting American presidents to two terms. The amendment, which was passed on March 21, 1947, prohibited anyone from being elected president more than twice. If a person served as president for more than two years of an unexpired term, that person could be elected to that office only once. An exception to this rule allowed the current president (President Truman), who had served two years of President Roosevelt's unexpired term, to be elected to two full terms in that office. Ratification was completed on February 27, 1951.

In 1952, Dwight D. Eisenhower, the Republican candidate, was elected president. Eisenhower, a former commander of the Allied military forces in Europe, was reelected in 1956. Many people believed Eisenhower, who was enormously popular, could have been elected to a third term in 1960 if the Twenty-second Amendment hadn't been adopted. (Democrats thought it was fitting that the Republicans, who had insisted on term limits for the president, should be the first to be caught in a trap of their own making.)

Although Eisenhower, who was seventy years old on October 14, 1960, was in good health at the time, he suffered serious health problems after becoming president. In 1955 he had a mild heart attack, but was able to carry out his duties while in the hospital. In 1956 he underwent an emergency operation for an intestinal disorder, but recovered quickly enough to run for reelection later in the year. In 1957 the president suffered a mild stroke that affected his speech temporarily. Although Eisenhower's health wasn't a factor in the 1960 election because he was prevented from seeking a third term under the Twenty-second Amendment, it was instrumental in the adoption of another amendment in 1967.

THE TWENTY-FIFTH AMENDMENT (1967)

SECTION 1. In case of the removal of the President from office or of his death or resignation, the Vice President shall become President.

SECTION 2. Whenever there is a vacancy in the office of the Vice President, the President shall nominate a Vice President who shall take office upon confirmation by a majority vote of both Houses of Congress.

SECTION 3. Whenever the President transmits to the President pro tempore of the Senate and the Speaker of the House of Representatives his written declaration that he is unable to discharge the powers and duties of his office, and until he transmits to them a written declaration to the contrary, such powers and duties shall be discharged by the Vice President as Acting President.

SECTION 4. Whenever the Vice President and a majority of either the principal officers of the executive departments or of such other body as Congress may by law provide, transmit to the President pro tempore of the Senate and the Speaker of the House of Representatives their written declaration that the President is unable to discharge the powers and duties of his office, the Vice President shall immediately assume the powers and duties of the office as Acting President.

Thereafter, when the President transmits to the President pro tempore of the Senate and the Speaker of the House of Representatives his written declaration that no inability exists, he shall resume the powers and duties of his office unless the Vice President and a majority of either the principal officers of the executive department or of such other body as Congress may by law provide, transmit within four days to the President pro tempore of the Senate and the Speaker of the House of Representatives their written declaration that the President is unable to discharge the powers and duties of his office. Thereupon Congress shall decide the issue, assembling within forty-eight hours for that purpose if not in session. If the Congress, within twenty-one days after receipt of the latter written declaration, or, if Congress is not in session, within twenty-one days after Congress is required to assemble, determines by two-thirds vote of both Houses that the President is unable to discharge the powers and duties of his office, the Vice President shall continue to discharge the same as acting President; otherwise, the President shall resume the powers and duties of his office.

There were several periods during which the United States had no vice president. Seven presidents died in office between 1841 and 1944, leaving the office of vice president vacant until the next presidential election. Moreover, a number of vice presidents died in office, and one, John C. Calhoun, resigned in 1832 to become a U.S. senator. To take care of such situations, Congress passed several presidential succession laws. Under the latest of these laws, which was passed in 1947, the order of presidential succession after the vice president is the speaker of the House, the president pro tempore of the Senate, and the various cabinet secretaries. This law has been amended several times to take into account changes in the executive departments, but the basic rules remain unchanged.

In the mid-1960s the country was mourning the death of a popular young president, John F. Kennedy, who was assassinated in Texas shortly before Thanksgiving in 1963. Kennedy's vice president, Lyndon Johnson, who became president after Kennedy's death and was elected to that office in 1964, was hospitalized for three days shortly after his 1965 inauguration. Kennedy's death and the illnesses of Eisenhower and Johnson prompted Congress to give serious thought to the issues of both presidential succession and a president's ability to handle the duties of that office. The result was the Twenty-fifth Amendment, which Congress passed on July 6, 1965. Ratification was completed on February 10, 1967.

The amendment provides that when the office of vice president becomes vacant, the president is to appoint someone to fill that office. After receiving a favorable vote from two-thirds of the members of each house of Congress, the new vice president assumes office. The amendment also allows the vice president to act as president temporarily when the president declares that he is unable to carry out his duties. Realizing that a president might fail to recognize his inability to function in that office because of severe illness or injury, for example, the amendment permits the vice president and the principal cabinet officials to inform Congress when they believe the president is unable to perform his duties. Congress then decides whether to allow the vice president to act as president or to permit the president to continue to carry out the duties of his office.

When the Twenty-fifth Amendment was adopted, no one anticipated that both a vice president and president would resign their offices within the space of a year. This happened in the early 1970s. In October 1973, President Richard M. Nixon's vice president, Spiro T. Agnew, resigned after pleading "no contest" to a charge of income tax evasion. Nixon named Republican Representative Gerald Ford of Michigan as Agnew's replacement, and Congress confirmed the appointment in December 1973. In August 1974, Nixon himself resigned because of mounting evidence of misconduct that seemed certain to result in his impeachment and removal from office. If the Twenty-fifth Amendment hadn't been in effect in 1973 to permit the appointment of a new vice president, Nixon, a Republican, would have been replaced as president by House Speaker Carl Albert, a Democrat.

FURTHER EXPANSIONS OF VOTING RIGHTS— AND AN AFTERTHOUGHT

In the ten-year period between 1961 and 1971 the Constitution was amended three times to expand people's voting rights. No further amendments were added until 1992, when a belated ratification of one of the twelve amendments passed by the First Congress made the Twenty-seventh Amendment part of the Constitution.

THE TWENTY-THIRD AMENDMENT (1961)

SECTION 1. The District constituting the seat of Government of the United States shall appoint in such manner as the Congress may direct:

A number of electors of President and Vice President equal to the whole number of Senators and Representatives in Congress to which the District would be entitled if it were a State, but in no event more than the least populous State; they shall be in addition to those appointed by the States, but they shall be considered, for the purposes of the election of President and Vice President, to be electors appointed by a State; and they shall meet in the District and perform such duties as provided by the twelfth article of amendment.

SECTION 2. The Congress shall have power to enforce this article by appropriate legislation.

The District of Columbia, the site of the nation's capital, isn't part of any state. This is because the framers of the Constitution were afraid that state politics would interfere with congressional decisions if the capital was located in one of the states. The First Congress established the district in 1790, using 100 square miles (260 square kilometers) of land along the banks of the Potomac River donated by the states of Maryland and Virginia for the new capital city. The major government buildings were erected on what had been the Maryland side of the river, and in 1846 the federal government returned to Virginia the land it had donated. Today much of the city of Washington is occupied by government or commercial buildings and by foreign embassies. However, the city also contains many residential neighborhoods where more than half a million people live.

As federally owned land, the District of Columbia is under the direct control of Congress as prescribed by Article I, Section 8, Clause 17 of the Constitution. For many years the residents of Washington, D.C., had little or no voice in the city's government. Moreover, they were unable to vote in national elections because they didn't live in one of the states. In 1871, Congress gave Washington limited self-government, but in 1874, after a scandal involving the local government, Congress resumed full control of its affairs.

Many people thought it was unfair that the people who lived in the capital city of a democratic country had so little opportunity to participate in their own government. However, the advocates of voting rights for residents of the city of Washington made little headway in persuading Congress to act on this issue until 1960. On June 17 of that year Congress passed the Twenty-third Amendment, giving the residents of the capital city the right to choose three electors for president and vice president. Most of the southern states opposed the amendment because they didn't want to give blacks, who made up more than half the city of Washington's population, voting rights. Only one southern state (Tennessee) ratified it before it was added to the Constitution on March 29, 1961.

In 1970, Congress allowed residents of the city of Washington to elect one nonvoting delegate to the House of Representatives, and in 1974 it gave the city limited self-government. Its residents can elect a mayor and city council, but the city's taxing authority is limited, and Congress retains overall supervision of the city's finances.

In August 1978, Congress passed a constitutional amendment that treated the District of Columbia as a state for purposes of national elections. The proposed amendment, which would have repealed the Twenty-third Amendment, gave the District two U.S. senators and one member of the House of Representatives. Congress included a seven-year period for the amendment's ratification by the states. At the end of the seven years, only sixteen states had ratified the amendment. After the rejection of the 1978 amendment, periodic attempts have been made to have the District of Columbia admitted as a fifty-first state. These attempts have been unsuccessful so far. Many people believe that statehood for the District of Columbia would result in the election of two black Democratic senators and at least one black Democratic House representative, depending on the city's population. This is because blacks, who now make up about three-quarters of the city's population, have shown an overwhelming tendency to vote Democratic since Washington regained limited home rule in 1974. Republicans, as well as those who still oppose black voting rights, thus have no inclination to support statehood for the District of Columbia.

For many years civil-rights activists tried to get Congress to pass a law outlawing the payment of poll taxes
as a requirement for voting (once a common practice in
the South). The opponents of poll taxes argued that
even though these taxes were small, they imposed a
disproportionate burden on blacks, who were often too
poor to pay them. Beginning in the 1940s the House of
Representatives passed several bills forbidding the use
of poll taxes as voting requirements for national elections, but the Senate failed to pass them.

In March 1962, President Kennedy announced his
support for a constitutional amendment banning the
payment of poll taxes as a requirement for voting in
national elections. The president's brother, Attorney
General Robert F. Kennedy, also supported the
amendment, although he believed Congress had the
authority to abolish poll taxes by passing a law. Despite some opposition by conservative southern senators, the proposed amendment passed the Senate by a
comfortable margin. The amendment ran into more
trouble in the House, where a number of Republicans
argued against it. Despite this opposition, the House
passed the amendment on August 27, 1962, by a small
margin.

Ratification of the Twenty-fourth Amendment was completed on January 23, 1964. At that time only five states (Alabama, Arkansas, Mississippi, Texas, and Virginia) still had poll tax laws in effect. While ratification was pending, Texas and Virginia passed laws providing for dual elections if the amendment should be adopted. These laws allowed all otherwise qualified persons to vote for federal officials but restricted voting for state and local officials to those who had paid the required tax.

In 1966 the Supreme Court struck down Virginia's new poll tax law. (A lower federal court had struck down the Texas law shortly before the Supreme Court ruled in the Virginia case.) The Court said in the case of *Harper* v. *Virginia Board of Elections* that the payment of fees was unrelated to the ability to participate intelligently in the electoral process. By distinguishing between rich and poor concerning the fundamental right to vote, the Virginia law introduced "a capricious or irrelevant factor" that violated the Fourteenth Amendment's equal protection clause.[6]

THE TWENTY-SIXTH AMENDMENT (1971)

SECTION 1. The right of citizens of the United States. who are eighteen years of age or older, to vote shall not be denied or abridged by the United States or by any State on account of age.

SECTION 2. The Congress shall have power to enforce this article by appropriate legislation.

The Voting Rights Act of 1965, which Congress passed to enforce the Fifteenth Amendment (see Chapter 7), forbade the use of literacy tests as a voting qualification for a five-year period in certain parts of the South. In

1970, while Congress was debating whether to extend the voting-rights law, three Democratic senators proposed amending the law to give voting rights to eighteen-year-olds. At that time the usual voting age was twenty-one, but four states (Alaska, Georgia, Hawaii, and Kentucky) allowed younger persons to vote, and several other states were considering whether to lower the voting age.

In 1970 many young Americans were protesting the country's involvement in a war in Vietnam, a small country in Southeast Asia. The United States had sent troops to Vietnam in the mid-1960s to stop North Vietnamese Communists from overruning South Vietnam. However, despite increasing involvement in the war the United States failed to dislodge the Communists from South Vietnam. The protests against the war, inspired in part by a draft of young men aged eighteen and over to serve in the military, had grown violent. The young protesters sometimes turned to rioting and arson to call attention to their demands that the United States get out of Vietnam. Faced with the prospect of continuing civil disorder, some political leaders began calling for voting rights for eighteen-year-olds. They reasoned that Americans who were old enough to fight in a war were old enough to vote. They also hoped that giving the young protesters the right to vote, and thereby a greater sense of control over their destinies, would curb antiwar demonstrations.

Senator Edward Kennedy of Massachusetts, one of the sponsors of the proposal, believed that Congress had the power to pass a law lowering the voting age. He based his conclusion on a Supreme Court decision regarding part of the 1965 voting-rights law. In 1966 the Court had upheld a provision of that law prohibiting the states from denying voting rights to persons who had completed at least six years of school in Puerto

Most of those who opposed the war in Vietnam, like these
demonstrators in Washington, D.C., in 1967,
were young people whose peers were being sent away
to fight. An eighteen-year-old, they pointed out, could
fight for his country, but was not allowed to
participate in its government. The Twenty-sixth
Amendment, which lowered the voting age to eighteen,
was based, in part, on this reasoning.

Rico (a U.S. commonwealth) because of their inability to read and write English. The provision affected many New York residents who had been educated in Puerto Rico, where classes were conducted in Spanish. The Court held that the law was a reasonable exercise of Congress's authority under the Fourteenth and Fifteenth Amendments. Senator Kennedy reasoned that Congress could pass a law giving voting rights to eighteen-year-olds based on the theory that a denial of voting rights to these persons violated their Fourteenth Amendment right to equal protection under the law, just as it had to those educated in Puerto Rico. Kennedy's reasoning, which was based on an article in a law school journal, persuaded Senate Majority Leader Mike Mansfield to include voting rights for eighteen-year-olds in the voting rights bill. (The other sponsor of the provision was Senator Warren Magnuson of Washington.)

Although many others disagreed with Senator Kennedy's interpretation of the Supreme Court decision, Congress added a provision on voting rights for eighteen-year-olds to the extension of the 1965 law. President Nixon, who shared the reservations about the authority of Congress to lower the voting age in the absence of a constitutional amendment, signed the bill anyway. In December 1970 the Supreme Court held by a five-to-four majority that while Congress had the authority to change the voting age for national elections, it did not have similar authority regarding state and local elections.

The Supreme Court's decision caused great concern in most states. A presidential election was less than two years away. Unless the states changed their rules on voting age (which often required amending the state constitution and submitting the amendment to the voters in a referendum), they would have to set up a mechanism for holding dual elections, as Texas and

Virginia had done while awaiting the ratification of the Twenty-fourth Amendment. Congress therefore rushed to pass another amendment forbidding the states from denying voting rights to otherwise qualified citizens aged eighteen and over. The Twenty-sixth Amendment, passed by Congress on March 23, 1971, was adopted on July 1, 1971, setting a record for speedy ratification.

Those who expected the new young voters to revolutionize elections were wrong. The votes of these young people haven't had any significant effect on national elections since 1972, the first year in which eighteen-year-olds in every state were eligible to vote in these elections.

AN AFTERTHOUGHT

As we have seen in Chapter 2, when Congress passed the first group of constitutional amendments in 1789, the states failed to ratify two of the twelve amendments. One dealt with the number of seats in the House of Representatives. The other dealt with changes in the compensation of members of Congress. Congress eventually settled the question of the number of House seats by passing a law that set the maximum number at 435, where it stands today. The question of pay raises for members of Congress was eventually settled by the ratification of the proposed amendment more than two hundred years after it was submitted to the states.

THE TWENTY-SEVENTH AMENDMENT (1992)
No law varying the compensation for the services of the Senators and Representatives shall take effect, until an election of Representatives shall have intervened.

After the proposed amendment regarding payment to members of Congress was submitted to the states in 1789, only six states had ratified it by 1800. The amendment was forgotten until 1873. In March 1873, the Republican Congress voted itself a retroactive pay raise. The Ohio legislature, angry over this "salary grab," promptly ratified the amendment. (Congress's act also resulted in the Democrats gaining control of Congress after the 1874 election.) No other state followed Ohio's example, however, so the amendment was once again forgotten until it was ratified by Wyoming in 1978.

During the 1980s a number of other states, concerned about the rising rate of compensation for members of Congress while the national debt had climbed to new heights, ratified the amendment. In 1989 seven states responded to a public outcry against a presidential advisory commission's recommended pay raise of about 50 percent for members of Congress by ratifying the amendment. (Both houses of Congress voted not to accept the pay raise, but the damage had already been done.) In 1990 two more states ratified the amendment, bringing the total number of ratifications to thirty-four.

In August 1991 the Senate added a pay raise of $23,000 for its members to a bill appropriating funds for Congress. The vote on the bill came at almost ten o'clock in the evening, after the network television newscasts had ended and the news deadlines for most major newspapers had passed. Although the pay raise was accompanied by restrictions on the amount of outside income the senators could earn, the seemingly stealthy act caused many complaints that the Senate had sneaked a pay raise past the public. One public interest spokesman called it "a pre-midnight raid on the taxpayers."[7] The public outrage caused four more states (Alabama, Missouri, New Jersey, and Michigan) to ratify the constitutional amendment. Ratification was completed on May 7, 1992. The amendment requires that changes in congressional pay apply only to members of future Congresses (including holdovers from previous Congresses).

The ratification of the Twenty-seventh Amendment surprised constitutional scholars as well as federal officials. Some questioned the validity of a ratification that took place so long after the amendment originally was presented to the states. Congress responded shortly after the amendment's adoption by proclaiming in an almost unanimous vote that it was now part of the Constitution.

The Twenty-seventh Amendment set a new record for delay in ratification. It is doubtful that this record will ever be broken. The other amendments that passed Congress but failed to be ratified have missed a deadline set for ratification or have been made obsolete by later events.

AMENDMENTS
THAT THE STATES
DID NOT RATIFY

Six of the thirty-three amendments that survived the congressional phase of the amendment process failed to achieve ratification. Three of these amendments have been discussed in previous chapters. They are the 1789 proposal to change the rule for the apportionment of seats in the House of Representatives (Chapter 12); the 1861 proposal to provide permanent protection for slavery in the states that still allowed it (Chapter 5); and the 1978 proposal to treat the District of Columbia as a state for purposes of representation in Congress (Chapter 12).

Another amendment that went unratified was approved by Congress in 1811. It provided that anyone who received a title of nobility or honor from a foreign country, or who accepted any monetary award from a foreign country, would lose his American citizenship and be permanently barred from holding any public office in the United States. Only a few states ratified this amendment, which has little or no practical significance today.

The two remaining unratified amendments illustrate the effect that changing Supreme Court interpretations of the Constitution can have on proposed constitutional amendments.

THE CHILD LABOR AMENDMENT

In 1924, Congress passed an amendment that would have given Congress as well as the states the authority to regulate or forbid the work of persons under the age of eighteen. The proposed child labor amendment was the result of a long and frustrating attempt to stop the practice of employing children in factories, mines, and other enterprises. Although many children worked on farms or in family-owned enterprises in our country's earlier period, by the end of the nineteenth century many people viewed the employment of children as a social evil that should be eliminated. A number of states passed laws restricting the work of children, but many believed that a federal law was needed to deal with the problem on a national basis.

In 1916, Congress passed a law forbidding the interstate transportation of goods made by child workers. The Supreme Court struck down this law in 1918 in the case of *Hammer* v. *Dagenhart.* The Court held in a five-to-four decision that the production of goods, even though they were intended for interstate commerce, was not in itself interstate commerce. The regulation of such production was a purely local matter, which was reserved to the states under the Tenth Amendment.

In 1919, Congress passed another law that imposed a tax on businesses that employed children under the age of fourteen or that required children between the ages of fourteen and sixteen to work more than eight hours a day or six days a week. In 1922 the Supreme Court struck down this law, too, by an eight-to-one majority. In the case of *Bailey* v. *Drexel Furniture Co.,* the Court concluded that the tax was really a penalty to force employers to restrict child labor, a matter that was solely the business of the state governments under the Tenth Amendment.

The two decisions prompted Congress to pass the 1924 child labor amendment. Although Presidents Calvin Coolidge, Herbert Hoover, and Franklin D. Roosevelt supported the amendment, it ran into trouble in the state legislatures, where manufacturing interests and conservative religious groups expressed opposition. The church groups were afraid that it would erode the authority of parents to compel their children to do household chores or help in family-owned businesses. By the time President Hoover left office in 1933, only eleven states had ratified the amendment.

The advent of the Great Depression and the high unemployment rate among adults increased public pressure for approval of the child labor amendment. As a result, fourteen states ratified it in 1933. It still needed to be ratified by eleven more states to become part of the Constitution, however. The country's main concern at that time was economic recovery, not social reform.

One of the earliest federal laws passed to encourage economic recovery during the 1930s was the National Industrial Recovery Act. This 1933 law called for agreements, or codes, to control the production and distribution of goods. One of these codes forbade the employment of children in the cotton textile industry, a major user of child labor. President Roosevelt hoped that the Supreme Court would uphold the 1933 law (and the resulting codes) as a valid way of dealing with the economic crisis. However, in 1935 the Supreme Court struck down the National Industrial Recovery Act in a unanimous decision. The Court held that business transactions that took place within one state did not constitute interstate commerce. Thus, Congress had no authority to regulate them. Although the decision didn't involve the textile industry code and its child labor ban, it invalidated both.

Before long, the Court struck down other new federal laws designed to combat the Depression. President Roosevelt and his advisers then looked for ways to overcome the Supreme Court's opposition to the new laws. The president first favored a constitutional amendment, but later decided that the problem was the Court, not the Constitution.

In February 1937, Roosevelt asked Congress for a law giving him the authority to appoint as many as six additional Supreme Court justices, one for each justice who stayed on the job more than six months after reaching the age of seventy. At that time six justices were over seventy. Four of the six were the Court's most conservative justices, who consistently ruled against the new economic recovery laws. The president's obvious attempt to "pack the Court" with sympathetic justices outraged many Americans, who viewed his action as an attack on the Constitution itself. Actually, Congress has the authority to change the number of Supreme Court justices, and has done so several times. However, because of the public outcry against it, Congress never passed Roosevelt's requested law.

Meanwhile, the child labor amendment was in trouble. In 1937 fourteen states rejected it. At that point an unexpected event occurred. Shortly after Roosevelt announced his "Court-packing" plan, the Supreme Court did an abrupt about-face. In a five-to-four decision the Court upheld the Wagner Labor Relations Act, which Congress had passed to replace the labor provisions of the National Industrial Recovery Act. The Court held that Congress had the authority to regulate business activities within a state if the activities had a close relationship to interstate commerce. This decision opened the door to another attempt to restrict child labor by a federal law based on Congress's power to regulate interstate commerce.

In 1938, Congress passed the Fair Labor Standards Act, which required minimum hourly wages and maximum weekly hours of work for employees engaged in the production of goods for interstate commerce. It also generally forbade the employment of children under the age of sixteen, or under eighteen in hazardous work. In 1941 the Supreme Court (a majority of whose justices by this time were Roosevelt appointees) upheld this law in a unanimous decision.

Today all states as well as the federal government have laws regulating child labor. Ratification of the child labor amendment was never completed because the Supreme Court's decision on the Fair Labor Standards Act made it unnecessary. In this instance President Roosevelt was right in concluding that a different Supreme Court would solve his problems without the need for a constitutional amendment.

THE EQUAL RIGHTS AMENDMENT

The campaign for a constitutional amendment to guarantee women the same rights as men began not long after the adoption of the Nineteenth Amendment (discussed in Chapter 9). Although women had the right to vote, many states still denied them the right to serve on juries, hold public office, control their own earnings without their husbands' consent, be appointed legal guardians, administer estates, make contracts, and receive the same pay as men for the same work. Alice Paul (the founder of the Woman's party) decided that the best way to fight these inequalities was to obtain another constitutional amendment. In 1923 she succeeded in having her equal rights amendment introduced in Congress.

Paul's amendment had few supporters, even among women. Most women's organizations and many prominent women reformers (including members of the Woman's party) opposed the amendment, believing it would do more harm than good.

Given such lack of support, Paul's proposed equal rights amendment fared poorly in Congress. In 1946 a majority of the U.S. Senate voted in favor of the amendment, but it failed to obtain the required two-thirds majority. Shortly after his election, President Kennedy revived the amendment when he appointed a commission to study all aspects of the status of women, including the need for an equal rights amendment. In its 1963 report the commission concluded that the amendment didn't appear to be necessary at that time. Instead, the commission endorsed the filing of lawsuits to test the idea that laws discriminating against women violated the Fourteenth Amendment's equal-protection clause.

In 1964, Congress included in its civil-rights law a section forbidding discrimination against women in employment. At first this provision was administered conservatively, but eventually it resulted in substantial progress for working women. Moreover, the lawsuits claiming that discrimination against women violated the Fourteenth Amendment eventually bore fruit. In a series of decisions during the 1970s the Supreme Court struck down a number of laws that gave preferential treatment to men over women as violations of that amendment's equal-protection clause.

Women's rights organizations, dissatisfied with the slow pace of reform, continued to push for a constitutional amendment. In March 1972, Congress passed the Equal Rights Amendment, which forbade both Congress and the states from denying or abridging the equality of rights on account of sex and gave Congress the power to enforce it by appropriate legislation. Congress included a seven-year period for ratification of the amendment, which would take effect two years after the date of its ratification.

Phyllis Schlafly, a conservative Republican, was instrumental in blocking the passage of the Equal Rights Amendment. The amendment's ratification period ended in 1982 after being extended for three additional years, and it died just three states short of being ratified.

Within one year of its passage, thirty-two states ratified it. However, organized opposition quickly sprang up. In October 1972, Phyllis Schlafly, a conservative Republican, formed the National Committee to Stop ERA. She argued that the amendment would endanger laws that exempted women from the obligation of military service and required husbands to support their wives (many of whom didn't work outside the home). She also pointed out that Congress's power to enforce the amendment could result in the transfer of authority to enact laws regarding family relations (marriage, divorce, child custody, and adoption) from the states to the federal government.

Schlafly's arguments were persuasive. Only three states ratified the amendment between 1973 and 1978. At that point it needed favorable votes from only three more states to become part of the Constitution. In 1978, however, two states that the amendment's supporters considered important (Virginia and Illinois) rejected it. Although Congress extended the period for ratification for another three years, the amendment died in 1982 after being ratified by thirty-five states, three short of the number needed to complete its ratification.

While the Equal Rights Amendment was under consideration in Congress, Senator Sam Ervin of North Carolina insisted that women's rights were adequately protected by the due process clause of the Fifth Amendment and the equal-protection clause of the Fourteenth Amendment. The Supreme Court's 1996 decision that the refusal of the Virginia Military Institute to admit women cadets violated the Fourteenth Amendment's equal-protection clause indicates that Senator Ervin may have been right, and that a further constitutional amendment to protect women isn't necessary.

OTHER PROPOSED AMENDMENTS

Most of the thousands of amendments that have been proposed since the Constitution was adopted have failed to win either the approval of two-thirds of the members of both houses of Congress or requests for a constitutional convention by two-thirds of the state legislatures. (Such a convention has never been held, although the states have come close to requiring Congress to call one at least twice in recent years.) Many of the unsuccessful attempts to amend the Constitution were quickly forgotten. Others, however, reflect controversies that are as old as the Constitution itself.

ELIMINATION OF THE ELECTORAL COLLEGE

The most commonly proposed amendment is one that would eliminate the electoral college, which chooses the president, and replace it with a system of direct election by the voters of the entire country. Many argue that the electoral-vote system is not only undemocratic but that it distorts the results of presidential elections by turning close popular votes into electoral vote landslides. This is because most states award electoral votes on a winner-take-all basis—the candidate with the highest number of popular votes receives all of that state's electoral votes. The electoral-vote system can also result in the election of a president who received fewer popular votes than his opponent. This has happened three times before. In the 1824 election Andrew Jackson received the largest number of both popular and electoral votes. But because the total number of votes was split among four candidates, Jackson failed to win a *majority* (more than 50 percent) of the electoral votes. The election was decided by the House of Representatives as provided by Article III, Section 2 of the Constitution and t he Twelfth Amendment. The House elected John Quincy Adams as president. Both Rutherford B. Hayes (elected in 1876) and Benjamin Harrison (elected in 1888) also received fewer popular votes than their opponents.

Despite these defects, Congress thus far has failed to pass a constitutional amendment to eliminate the electoral college. Why haven't we eliminated it? The primary reason may be that, despite its flaws, the electoral-vote system doesn't generally cause problems. It also has one advantage—it reinforces the two-party system by hindering the two major parties from breaking up into splinter parties, which would have a hard time winning a majority of electoral votes. Moreover, both major parties have learned how to use it to their best advantage in presidential elections, and thus see no compelling reason for changing it. It seems likely, therefore, that unless a future presidential election produces a grossly unfair result, we will continue to follow what almost everyone agrees is a cumbersome, outmoded, and undemocratic method of selecting an American president.

APPORTIONMENT OF STATE LEGISLATURES

The Constitution requires that seats in the U.S. House of Representatives be apportioned (that is, divided into proportional shares) according to the country's population, to be calculated by a census held every ten years. The Constitution says nothing about how the apportionment is to be done, or about the assignment of seats in the state legislatures. The delegates to the 1787 convention assumed that this latter question was a matter for each state to decide. After the adoption of the Constitution, Congress generally left it up to the states to decide how to apportion their congressional seats as long as they came up with the required number of seats.

For many years the Supreme Court refused to hear apportionment cases on the grounds that these were political issues on which it had no authority to decide. Meanwhile, the failure of many state legislatures to reallocate their own legislative districts and their congressional districts in keeping with changing populations led to serious imbalances in these bodies. In some instances the populations of the growing urban districts were many times larger than those in rural areas.

In the early 1960s the Court reversed its previous conclusion and decided to hear several cases involving the apportionment issue. It then held that state legislative districts and congressional districts (the districts established for purposes of House representation) must be roughly equal in population—the so-called one person, one vote doctrine. The Court's decisions were based on a finding that the unequal distribution of representation violated the equal-protection clause of the Fourteenth Amendment.

In 1964 the Court held that the equal-protection clause requires that the seats in both houses of state legislatures must be apportioned on a population basis. The decision meant that many states, which assigned their Senate seats according to political subdivisions (usually counties), had to reorganize their legislatures. This caused a public outcry. In 1965, Senator Everett M.

(145)

Dirksen of Illinois introduced an amendment that would have allowed states to apportion seats in one house of their legislature on a basis other than population. After the proposal failed to receive a two-thirds majority in the Senate, Senator Dirksen actively supported a drive for a constitutional convention to consider his proposed amendment. By June 1969, thirty-three states (only one less than the two-thirds majority needed to compel Congress to call a constitutional convention) had asked for such a convention. However, opponents warned about the dangers of a "runaway" convention, which might overturn the entire Constitution. The warnings caused North Carolina to rescind (withdraw) its request for a constitutional convention. Dirksen's death in September 1969 ended the campaign.

PRAYER IN PUBLIC SCHOOLS

In the early 1960s the Supreme Court banned the use of officially sponsored prayers and Bible readings in public schools as unconstitutional establishments of religion. The decisions outraged many Americans, especially members of conservative Christian churches, who viewed the Court's rulings as attempts to remove God from the nation's schools. (The fact that one decision was the result of a lawsuit by avowed atheists—persons who don't believe there is a God—reinforced this belief.) Since that time, numerous resolutions have been introduced in Congress calling for a constitutional amendment to allow both prayers and Bible readings in public schools. The school prayer amendment is controversial, however. A number of religious leaders oppose it. Because there appears to be no nationwide consensus on the issue, Congress has failed to achieve the two-thirds majority needed to pass a school prayer amendment.

ABORTION

In 1973 the Supreme Court issued a decision striking down state laws that banned most abortions. The Court held in the case of *Roe* v. *Wade* that a Texas abortion law violated the Fourteenth Amendment's due-process clause. It also based its ruling on a right of privacy, which is not specifically mentioned in the Constitution. Although the Court affirmed the state's legitimate interest in protecting both the expectant mother and the developing fetus in the later stages of pregnancy, it declined to rule that the fetus is a "person" entitled to Fourteenth Amendment protection.

The decision caused an immediate uproar. Members of conservative groups, who viewed abortion as murder, denounced it for giving government approval to wrongful acts. Some constitutional-law scholars also criticized the decision, which they thought was based on vague and flimsy grounds. The Supreme Court itself remains divided on this issue. Subsequent decisions have upheld restrictions to a woman's right to an abortion, but the Court has refused to overturn the 1973 decision. Moreover, Congress has not passed a constitutional amendment outlawing abortions.

FLAG BURNING

Most states in the past had laws forbidding the desecration or misuse of the American flag. These laws became a constitutional issue in the late 1960s, when antiwar protesters burned or trampled on the flag to show their opposition to American involvement in the Vietnam War. During that period the Supreme Court struck down several state laws regarding flag desecration because they were too vague or because they interfered with the First Amendment guarantee of free speech.

Abortion is an issue that divides many Americans, including the justices of the Supreme Court. Abortion laws have been upheld or restricted based on Constitutional amendments, but so far no amendment has been passed to outlaw abortions. This demonstrator in 1978 shows that she, like many people, feels that government has no right to limit such decisions.

In 1989 the controversy over flag burning erupted again when the Supreme Court reversed the conviction of a man who had burned an American flag as a political protest. The Court held in a five-to-four decision that the man's conviction violated his right of free speech. The furor over the decision resulted in Congress's passage of a Flag Protection Act, which forbade anyone from knowingly defiling the flag. The Court struck this law down in 1990 in another close decision. Afterward, two flag protection amendments were introduced in Congress, but failed to win approval. In June 1997 the House passed a third flag protection amendment, but so far the Senate has failed to act on it. Most Americans view the disrespectful treatment of the flag as a despicable act. The legislatures of forty-nine states have responded to this public sentiment by urging Congress to approve a flag protection amendment. However, opponents of the amendment argue that such conduct occurs so infrequently that a constitutional amendment seems unnecessary. They also fear that such an amendment might result in an unintended infringement of our First Amendment right to freedom of speech in areas other than showing disrespect for the flag.

TERM LIMITS FOR MEMBERS OF CONGRESS

The question of term limits for members of Congress predates the 1787 convention. The Articles of Confederation limited members of Congress to three years of service in any six-year period. The Virginia Plan introduced early in the 1787 convention proposed limiting members of Congress to a single term of office. The proposal was later dropped. However, the Anti-Federalists brought up the issue again during the ratification period. The Anti-Federalist writer Brutus expressed the opinion that senators once chosen would probably continue in office for life, since long-term senators were likely to be removed only for gross misconduct.

History has since borne out Brutus's prediction. For example, Senator Strom Thurmond of South Carolina has been a senator for more than forty years. Four current U.S. senators have held this office for more than thirty years, and more than a dozen have been in office at least twenty years. Moreover, most long-term senators eventually leave office through retirement instead of being defeated in a bid for reelection.

In recent years evidence of corruption and abuse of power by members of Congress, and complaints that these officials are out of touch with the voters, sparked a drive for term limits for these officials. Almost two dozen states passed laws that imposed term limits on their representatives in Congress. In 1995 the Supreme Court struck down these laws in a five-to-four decision. The Court held that the states may not impose greater restrictions on the terms of members of Congress than the Constitution itself imposes. Advocates of term limits then tried to get a constitutional amendment that would limit members of Congress to twelve years in office (two terms in the Senate and six terms in the House of Representatives). So far the proposed amendment has not received congressional approval.

In November 1996 the voters in nine states approved measures that would require their legislatures to ask Congress for a constitutional convention to consider the proposed term-limits amendment, but four other states rejected similar proposals. Moreover, Congress has shown little interest in passing amendments that might put many of its members out of office.

BALANCED BUDGETS

The notion of requiring the federal government to balance its budget is also as old as the Constitution. In

January 1788, Brutus warned that giving Congress the power to borrow money could result in a national debt so large that it would be impossible to ever repay it—a prediction that many believe is close to being realized. Many Americans, concerned about the rising national debt and the constant squabbles over the federal budget, began calling for a constitutional amendment to require a balanced budget. When Congress failed to act on these proposals, the amendment's supporters turned to the state legislatures for action. By the mid-1980s, thirty-two states had asked Congress to call a constitutional convention to discuss this issue.

In the 1994 election the Republicans took control of both houses of Congress, something that hadn't happened since 1952. The new Republican House of Representatives promptly fulfilled a campaign promise by passing a balanced budget amendment in January 1995. However, in March of that year the amendment failed by one vote to win approval in the Senate. In 1996 the Senate again defeated the proposed amendment, this time by a margin of three votes. In March 1997 the Senate defeated the amendment by one vote.

DO WE NEED A NEW CONSTITUTION?

Most Americans revere the Constitution, now enshrined in the nation's capital in a glass-enclosed case to protect the fragile parchment. Some day, however, the parchment will disintegrate despite the best efforts to preserve it. Will we also decide some day to discard the Constitution instead of continuing to patch it with new amendments?

Most of the Constitution, which was written to solve problems that have long since disappeared, is admittedly obsolete. Parts of it are also hard to understand. One constitutional scholar has recently characterized the Constitution as "elusive, ambiguous, murky, sometimes quite opaque." He also points out that the Constitution, which he describes as "a charter of shimmering truths and obscurities," has lasted this long precisely because of these characteristics.[8]

Perhaps the late Supreme Court Justice William J. Brennan, Jr., said it best. In a speech written to commemorate the two-hundredth anniversary of the Constitution Justice Brennan said, "Our entire Constitution is a national treasure: a document of heady ideals and eloquent, elegant language; a political landmark for individual rights. But one thing the old parchment is not is a china doll that has to be protected from the regular world by a good layer of cotton wool. It is a tough old soldier that's collected quite a few respectable dents in the line of duty."[9]

In 1787 a small group of men, prompted by a sense of crisis, overcame their diversity of interests to produce the Constitution. Today the nation has reached a size and degree of diversity no one could have predicted in 1787. Moreover, although we remain deeply divided on many issues, no crisis seems to threaten our national existence. It seems likely, therefore, that even if we should have a new constitutional convention, it won't result in a new Constitution. Instead, we will probably decide to keep the old one, just as we keep that shabby but comfortable pair of old sneakers that we refuse to throw away. Like those cherished sneakers, the Constitution is still usable, although patched and somewhat out of fashion. And there is always the danger that its replacement, while shiny and new, might pinch our feet.

THE CONSTITUTION OF THE UNITED STATES

PREAMBLE

We the people of the United States, in order to form a more perfect union, establish justice, insure domestic tranquility, provide for the common defense, promote the general welfare, and secure the blessings of liberty to ourselves and our posterity, do ordain and establish this Constitution for the United States of America.

ARTICLE I

SECTION 1

All legislative powers herein granted shall be vested in a Congress of the United States, which shall consist of a Senate and House of Representatives.

SECTION 2

The House of Representatives shall be composed of members chosen every second year by the people of the several states, and the electors in each state shall have the qualifications requisite for electors of the most numerous branch of the state legislature.

No person shall be a representative who shall not have attained to the age of twenty-five years, and been seven years a citizen of the United States, and who shall not, when elected, be an inhabitant of that state in which he shall be chosen.

Representatives and direct taxes shall be apportioned among the several states which may be included within this union, according to their respective numbers, which shall be determined by adding to the whole number of free persons, including those bound to service for a term of years, and excluding Indians not taxed, three-fifths of all other persons. The actual enumeration shall be made within three years after the first meeting of the Congress of the United States, and within every subsequent term of ten years, in such manner as they shall be law direct. The number of representatives shall not exceed one for every thirty thousand, but each state shall have at least one representative; and until such enumeration shall be made, the state of New Hampshire shall be entitled to choose three, Massachusetts eight, Rhode Island and Providence Plantations one, Connecticut five, New York six, New Jersey four, Pennsylvania eight, Delaware one, Maryland six, Virginia ten, North Carolina five, South Carolina five, and Georgia three.

When vacancies happen in the representation of any state, the executive authority thereof shall issue writs of election to fill such vacancies. The House of Representatives shall choose their speaker and other officers; and shall have the sole power of impeachment.

SECTION 3
The Senate of the United States shall be composed of two senators from each state, chosen by the legislature thereof, for six years and each senator shall have one vote.

Immediately after they shall be assembled in consequence of the first election, they shall be divided as equally as may be into three classes. The seats of senators of the first class shall be vacated at the expiration of the second year, of the second class at the expiration of the fourth year, and of the third class at the expiration of the sixth year, so that one-third may be chosen every second year; and if vacancies happen by resignation, or otherwise, during the recess of the legislature of any state, the executive thereof may make temporary appointments until the next meeting of the legislature, which shall then fill such vacancies.

No person shall be a senator who shall not have attained to the age of thirty years, and been nine years a citizen of the United States, and who shall not, when elected, be an inhabitant of that state for which he shall be chosen.

The vice president of the United States shall be president of the Senate, but shall have no vote, unless they be equally divided.

The Senate shall choose their other officers, and also a president pro tempore, in the absence of the vice president, or when he shall exercise the office of president of the United States.

The Senate shall have the sole power to try all impeachments. When sitting for that purpose, they shall be on oath or affirmation. When the president of the United States is tried, the chief justice shall preside: and no person shall be convicted without the concurrence of two thirds of the members present.

Judgment in the cases of impeachment shall not extend further than to removal from office, and disqualification to hold and enjoy any office of honor, trust, or profit under the United States: but the party convicted shall nevertheless be liable and subject to indictment, trial, judgment, and punishment, according to law.

SECTION 4
The times, places, and manner of holding elections for senators and representatives, shall be prescribed in each state by the legislature thereof; but the Congress may at any time by law make or alter such regulations, except as to the places of choosing senators.

The Congress shall assemble at least once in every year, and such meeting shall be on the first Monday in December, unless they shall by law appoint a different day.

SECTION 5
Each house shall be the judge of the elections, returns, and qualifications of its own members, and a majority of each shall constitute a quorum to do business; but a small number may adjourn from day to day, and may be authorized to compel the attendance of absent members, in such manner, and under such penalties as each house may provide.

Each house may determine the rules of its proceedings, punish its members for disorderly behaviour, and, with the concurrence of two thirds, expel a member.

Each house shall keep a journal of its proceedings, and from time to time publish the same, excepting such parts as may in their judgment require secrecy; and the yeas and the nays of the members of either house on any question shall, at the desire of one-fifth of those present, be entered on the journal.

Neither house, during the session of Congress, shall, without the consent of the other, adjourn for more than three days, nor to any other place other than that in which the two houses shall be sitting.

SECTION 6

The senators and representatives shall receive a compensation for their services, to be ascertained by law, and paid out of the treasury of the United States. They shall in all cases, except treason, felony, and breach of the peace, be privileged from arrest during their attendance at the session of their respective houses, and in going to and returning from the same; and for any speech or debate in either house, they shall not be questioned in any other place.

No senator or representative shall, during the time for which he was elected, be appointed to any civil office under the authority of the United States, which shall have been created, or the emoluments whereof shall have been increased during such time; and no person holding any office under the United States, shall be a member of either house during his continuance in office.

SECTION 7

All bills for raising revenue shall originate in the House of Representatives; but the Senate may propose or concur with amendments as on other bills.

Every bill which shall have passed the House of Representatives and the Senate, shall, before it becomes law, be presented to the president of the United States; if he approves he shall sign it, but if not he shall return it, with his objections to that house in which it shall have originated, who shall enter the objections at large on their journal, and proceed to reconsider it. If after such reconsideration two thirds of that house shall agree to pass the bill, it shall be sent, together with the objections, to the other house, by which it shall likewise be reconsidered, and if approved by two thirds of that house, it shall become a law. But in all such cases the votes of both houses shall be determined by yeas and nays, and the names of the persons voting for and against the bill shall be entered on the journal of each house respectively. If any bill shall not be returned by the president within ten days (Sundays excepted) after it shall have been presented to him, the same shall be a law, in like manner as if head signed it, unless the Congress by their adjournment prevent its return, in which case it shall not be a law.

Every order, resolution, or vote to which the concurrence of the Senate and House of Representatives may be necessary (except in question of adjournment) shall be presented to the president of the United States; and before the same shall take effect, shall be approved by him, or being disapproved by him, shall be repassed by two thirds of the Senate and

House of Representatives, according to the rules and limitations prescribed in the case of a bill.

SECTION 8

The Congress shall have power to lay and collect taxes, duties, imposts, and excises, to pay the debts and provide for the common defense and general welfare of the United States; but all duties, imposts, and excises shall be uniform throughout the United States:

To borrow money on the credit of the United States;

To regulate commerce with foreign nations, and among the several states, and with the Indian tribes;

To establish a uniform rule of naturalization, and uniform laws on the subject of bankruptcies throughout the United States;

To coin money, regulate the value thereof, and of foreign coin, and fix the standard of weights and measures;

To provide for the punishment of counterfeiting the securities and current coin of the United States;

To establish post offices and post roads;

To promote the progress of science and useful arts, by securing for limited times to authors and inventors the exclusive right to their respective writings and discoveries;

To constitute tribunals inferior to the Supreme Court;

To define and punish piracies and felonies committed on the high seas, and offenses against the law of nations;

To declare war, grant letters of marque and reprisal, and make rules concerning captures on land and water;

To raise and support armies, but no appropriation of money to that use shall be for a longer term than two years;

To provide and maintain a navy;

To make rules for the government and regulation of the land and naval forces;

To provide for calling forth the militia to execute the laws of the union, suppress insurrections, and repel invasions;

To provide for organizing, arming, and disciplining the militia, and for governing such part of them as may be employed in the service of the United States, reserving to the states respectively, the appointment of the officers, and the authority of training the militia according to the discipline prescribed by Congress;

To exercise legislations in all cases whatsoever, over such district (not exceeding ten miles square) as may, by cession of particular states, and the acceptance of Congress, become the seat of the government of the United States, and to exercise like authority over all places purchased by the consent of the legislature of the state in which the same shall be, for the erection of forts, magazines, arsenals, dock-yards, and other needful buildings; And

To make all laws which shall be necessary and proper for carrying into execution the foregoing powers, and all other powers vested by this Constitution in the government of the United States, or in any department or officer thereof.

SECTION 9

The migration or importation of such persons as any of the states now existing shall think proper to admit, shall not be prohibited by the Congress prior to the year one thousand eight hundred and eight, but a tax or duty may be imposed on such importation, not exceeding ten dollars for each person.

The privilege of the writ of habeas corpus shall not be suspended, unless when in cases of rebellion or invasion the public safety may require it.

No bill of attainder or ex post facto law shall be passed.

No capitation, or other direct, tax shall be laid, unless in proportion to the census or enumeration herein before directed to be taken.

No tax or duty shall be laid on articles exported from any state.

No preference shall be given by any regulation of commerce or revenue to the ports of one state over those of another: nor shall vessels bound to, or from, one state, be obliged to enter, clear, or pay duties in another.

No money shall be drawn from the treasury, but in consequence of appropriations made by law; and a regular statement and account of the receipts and expenditures of all public money shall be published from time to time.

No title of nobility shall be granted by the United States: and no person holding any office of profit or trust under them, shall, without the consent of the Congress, accept of any present, emolument, office, or title, of any kind whatever, from any king, prince, or foreign state.

SECTION 10

No state shall enter into any treaty, alliance, or confederation; grant letters of marque and reprisal; coin money; emit bills of credit; make any thing but gold and silver coin a tender in payment of debts; pass any bill of attainder, ex post facto law, or law impairing the obligation of contracts, or grant any title of nobility.

No state shall, without the consent of the Congress, lay any imposts or duties on imports or exports, except what may be absolutely necessary for executing its inspection laws; and the net produce of all duties and imports, laid by any state on imports or exports, shall be for the use of the treasury of the United States; and all such laws shall be subject to the revision and control of the Congress.

No state shall, without the consent of Congress, lay any duty of tonnage, keep troops, or ships of war in time of peace, enter into any agreement or compact with any other state, or with a foreign power, or engage in war, unless actually invaded, or in such imminent danger as will not admit of delay.

ARTICLE II

SECTION 1

The executive power shall be vested in a president of the United States of America. He shall hold his office during the term of four years, and together with the vice president, chosen for the same term, be elected, as follows: Each state shall appoint, in such manner as the legislature thereof may direct, a number of electors, equal to the whole number of senators and representatives to which the state may be entitled in the Congress; but no senator or representative, or person holding an office of trust or profit under the United States, shall be appointed by an elector.

The electors shall meet in the respective states, and vote by ballot for two persons, of whom one at least shall not be an inhabitant of the same state with themselves. And they shall make a list of all the persons voted for, and of the number of votes for each; which list they shall sign and certify, and transmit sealed to the seat of government of the United States, directed to the president of the Senate. The president of the Senate shall, in the presence of the Senate and House of Representatives, open all the certificates, and the votes shall then be counted. The person having the greatest number of votes shall be the president, if such number be a majority of the whole number of electors appointed; and if there be more than one who have such majority, and have an equal number of votes, then the House of Representatives shall immediately choose by ballot one of them for president, and if no person have a majority, then from the five highest on the list the said House shall in like manner choose the president. But in choosing the president, the votes shall be taken by states, the representation from each state having one vote; a quorum for this purpose shall consist of a member or members from two thirds of the states, and a majority of all the states shall be necessary to a choice. In every case, after the choice of the president, the person having the greatest number of votes of the electors shall be the vice president. But if there should remain two or more who have equal votes, the Senate shall choose from them by ballot the vice president.

The Congress may determine the time of choosing the electors, and the day on which they shall give their votes; which day shall be the same throughout the United States.

No person except a natural born citizen, or a citizen of the United States, at the time of the adoption of this Constitution, shall be eligible to the office of the president; neither shall any person be eligible to that office who shall not have attained to the age of thirty-five years, and been fourteen years a resident within the United States.

In case of the removal of the president from office, or of his death, resignation, or inability to discharge the powers and duties of the said office, the same shall devolve on the vice president, and the Congress may by law provide for the case of removal, death, resignation, or inability, both of the president and vice president, declaring what officer shall then act as president, and such officer shall act accordingly, until the disability removed, or a president be elected.

The president shall, at stated times, receive for his services, a compensation, which shall neither be increased nor diminished during the period for which he shall have been elected, and he shall not receive within that period any other emolument from the United States, or any of them.

Before he enter on the execution of his office, he shall take the following oath or affirmation: "I do solemnly swear (or affirm) that I will faithfully execute the office of president of the United States, and will to the best of my ability, preserve, protect, and defend the Constitution of the United States."

SECTION 2

The president shall be commander in chief of the army and navy of the United States, and of the militia of the several states, when called into the actual service of the United States; he may require the opinion, in writing, of the principal officer in each of the executive departments, upon any subject relating to the duties of their respective offices, and he shall have power to grant reprieves and pardons for offenses against the United States, except in cases of impeachment.

He shall have power, by and with the advice and consent of the Senate, to make treaties, provided two thirds of the Senators present concur; and he shall nominate, and by and with the advice and consent of the Senate, shall appoint ambassadors, other public ministers and consuls, judges of the Supreme Court, and all other officers of the United States, whose appointments are not herein otherwise provided for, and which shall be established by law; but the Congress may by law vest the appointment of such inferior officers, as they think proper, in the President alone, in the courts of law, or in the heads of departments.

The president shall have the power to fill up all vacancies that may happen during the recess of the Senate, by granting commissions which shall expire at the end of their next session.

SECTION 3

He shall from time to time give to the Congress information of the state of the union, and recommend to their consideration such measures as he shall judge necessary and expedient; he may, on extraordinary occasions, convene both houses, or either of them, and in case of disagreement between them, with respect to the time of adjournment, he may adjourn them to such time as he shall think proper; he shall receive ambassadors and other public ministers; he shall take care that the laws be faithfully executed, and shall commission all the officers of the United States.

SECTION 4

The president, vice president, and all civil officers of the United States, shall be removed from office on impeachment for, and conviction of, treason, bribery, or other high crimes and misdemeanors.

ARTICLE III

SECTION 1

The judicial power of the United States, shall be vested in one Supreme Court, and in such inferior courts as the Congress may from time to time ordain and establish. The judges, both of the Supreme and inferior courts, shall hold their offices during good behaviour, and shall, at stated times, receive for their services, a compensation, which shall not be diminished during their continuance in office.

SECTION 2

The judicial power shall extend to all cases, in law and equity, arising under this Constitution, the laws of the United States, and treaties made, or which shall be made, under their authority; to all cases affecting ambassadors, other public ministers and consuls; to all cases of admiralty and maritime jurisdiction; to controversies to which the United States shall be a party; to controversies between two or more states; between a state and citizens of another state; between citizens of different states; between citizens of the same state claiming lands under grants of different states, and between a state, or the citizens thereof, and foreign states, citizens, or subjects.

In all cases affecting ambassadors, other public ministers and consuls, and those in which a state shall be a party, the Supreme Court shall have original jurisdiction. In all the other cases before mentioned, the Supreme Court shall have appellate jurisdiction, both as to law and fact, with such exceptions, and under such regulations as the Congress shall make.

The trial of all crimes, except in cases of impeachment, shall be by jury; and such trial shall be held in the state where the said crimes shall have been committed; but when not committed within any state, the trial shall be at such place or places as the Congress by law have directed.

SECTION 3

Treason against the United States, shall consist only in levying war against them, or in adhering to their enemies, giving them aid and comfort. No person shall be convicted of treason unless on the testimony of two witnesses to the same overt act, or on confession in open court.

The Congress shall have power to declare the punishment of treason, but no attainder of treason shall work corruption of blood, or forfeiture except during the life of the person attainted.

ARTICLE IV

SECTION 1

Full faith and credit shall be given in each state to the public acts, records, and judicial proceedings of every other state. And the Congress may by general laws prescribe the manner in which such acts, records, and proceedings shall be proved, and the effect thereof.

SECTION 2

The citizens of each state shall be entitled to all privileges and immunities of citizens in the several states.

A person charged in any state with treason, felony, or other crime, who shall flee from justice, and be found in another state, shall on demand of the executive authority of the state from which he fled, be delivered up, to be removed to the state having jurisdiction of the crime.

No person held to service or labour in one state, under the laws thereof, escaping into another, shall in consequence of any law or regulation therein, be discharged from such service or labour, but shall be delivered up on claim of the party to whom such service or labour may be due.

SECTION 3

New states may be admitted by the Congress into this union; but no new state shall be formed or erected within the jurisdiction of any other state; nor any state be formed by the junction of two or more states, or parts of states, without the consent of the legislatures of the states concerned as well as of the Congress.

The Congress shall have power to dispose of and make all needful rules and regulations respecting the territory or other property belonging to the United States, or of any particular state.

SECTION 4

The United States shall guarantee to every state in this union a republican form of government, and shall protect each of them against invasion; and on application of the legislature, or of the executive (when the legislature cannot be convened) against domestic violence.

ARTICLE V

The Congress, whenever two thirds of both houses shall deem it necessary, shall propose amendments to this Constitution, or on the application of the legislature of two thirds of the several states, shall call a convention for proposing amendments, which, in either case, shall be valid to all intents and purposes, as part of this Constitution, when ratified by the legislatures of three fourths of the several states, or by conventions in three fourths thereof, as the one or the other mode of ratification may be proposed by the Congress; provided that no amendment which may be made prior to the year one thousand eight hundred and eight shall in any manner affect the first and fourth clauses in the ninth section of the first article; and that no state, without its consent, shall be deprived of equal suffrage in the Senate.

ARTICLE VI

All debts contracted and engagements entered into, before the adoption of this Constitution, shall be as valid against the United States under this Constitution, as under the confederation.

This Constitution, and the laws of the United States which shall be made in pursuance thereof; and all treaties made, or which shall be made, under the authority of the United States, shall be the supreme law of the land; and the judges in every state shall be bound thereby, any thing in the Constitution or laws of any state to the contrary notwithstanding.

The senators and representatives before mentioned, and the members of the several state legislatures, and all executive and judicial officers, both of the United States and of the several states, shall be bound by oath or affirmation, to support this Constitution; but no religious test shall ever be required as a qualification to any office or public trust under the United States.

ARTICLE VII

The ratification of the conventions of the nine states shall be sufficient for the establishment of this Constitution between the states so ratifying the same.

Done in convention by the unanimous consent of the states present the seventeenth day of September in the year of our Lord one thousand seven hundred and eighty seven and of the independence of the United States of America the twelfth. In witness whereof we have hereunto subscribed our names,

NOTES

1. Doyle Mathis, "Chisholm v. Georgia: Background and Settlement," *Journal of American History*, vol. 54 (June 1967), pp.19-29.

2. 2 Dall. 419 (U.S. 1793) at 456.

3. 392 U.S. 409 (1968) at 443.

4. Eric Foner, *Reconstruction, 1863-1877: America's Unfinished Revolution* (New York: Harper & Row, 1988), p. 76.

5. Malcolm M. Feeley and Samuel Krislow, *Constitutional Law* (Boston: Little, Brown & Co., 1985), pp. 165-166.

6. 383 U.S. 663 (1966) at 668.

7. *Facts on File*, 1991: 543B1.

8. Jethro K. Lieberman, *The Evolving Constitution* (New York: Random House, 1992), pp. 12, 19.

9. *Baltimore Sun*, July 25, 1997, p. 16A.

GLOSSARY

abridge—to restrict or reduce in scope.

amendment—a formal process of changing an official document. Changes in the U.S. Constitution are called amendments.

Anti-Federalist—a person who opposed the ratification of the Constitution.

appellate jurisdiction—the power to review court decisions. The Supreme Court has this power of review over decisions of lower federal courts and state courts on questions involving the Constitution or federal laws.

apportionment—a division or allotment into proportionate shares, such as seats in a legislative body according to population.

bill of rights—a formal statement of the rights and privileges that are protected against infringement by the government. The first ten amendments to the Constitution are called the Bill of Rights.

civil rights—the legal ability to deal equally with others in society, such as the ability to make contracts, own property, start lawsuits, and testify in court. The term does not ordinarily mean the right to vote, which is considered a political right.

constitution—a written document establishing the basic rules of an organization. The U.S. Constitution sets out the general rules under which the national government operates.

direct taxes—as used in the Constitution, the term means taxes that must be apportioned according to population.

dissent—a difference of opinion. A Supreme Court justice who disagrees with the majority's opinion usually writes a dissenting opinion.

due process of law—a term that generally means an established procedure designed to ensure fairness. The term, which is not defined in the Constitution, has been interpreted by courts in different and sometimes conflicting ways.

duties—taxes imposed on goods imported from another country.

electoral college—the group that elects the president and vice president of the United States.

electoral votes—the votes cast by members of the electoral college.

eminent domain—the power of the government to take private property for public use. The Constitution requires that in such a taking the property owner must receive fair compensation.

excise—a tax imposed on the manufacture, sale, or consumption of a product made in the United States.

exclusionary rule—a rule that forbids the use of unlawfully obtained evidence in criminal trials.

executive branch—the branch of the federal government that is responsible for executing, or carrying out, the laws passed by Congress. The president, his staff, and the officials and employees of the various federal departments and agencies are part of the executive branch.

federal government—the national government of the United States.

federalism—a system of government in which power is divided between the states and the central government, with each having control over specific areas of government.

Federalist—a person who supported the Constitution during the ratification period. The term also refers to a member of the Federalist party.

grand jury—a body of citizens that decides whether there is enough evidence to order persons to be brought to trial for criminal offenses.

grandfather clause—a provision that exempts certain persons from following newly established requirements. Grandfather clauses were often used in the South to exempt whites from new rules that imposed stricter requirements for voting.

impost—a duty or tax imposed on goods imported from other countries.

indictment—a formal written accusation against a person who is suspected of committing a crime.

judicial branch—the branch of the federal government responsible for interpreting the laws and the Constitution and for hearing and reviewing cases involving federal laws and the Constitution. The federal courts are part of the judicial branch.

jurisdiction—the authority to govern, to make laws, or to interpret them. The term also refers to the limits or geographic areas within which authority may be exercised.

jury—a body of citizens that weighs the evidence presented during a trial and reaches a conclusion, or verdict, on a particular question.

legislative branch—the branch of the federal government responsible for making national laws. The Constitution gives Congress the federal government's legislative or lawmaking power.

original jurisdiction—the authority to handle a case at its origin instead of reviewing the decisions of other courts. In certain cases the Supreme Court has original jurisdiction—that is, it acts as a trial court, hearing evidence and reaching a conclusion.

poll tax—a tax imposed on individuals. Poll taxes are also called head taxes or capitation taxes. The imposition of poll taxes as requirements for voting has been outlawed by the Twenty-fourth Amendment and by a Supreme Court decision.

privileges and immunities—the Constitution does not define this term. The courts have held that it applies to such rights as the right to travel from one state to another, to petition Congress, and to vote in national elections. The Constitution's privileges and immunities provisions also prevent states from discriminating against residents of other states.

probable cause—this term is used in the Fourth Amendment to prevent searches without good reason that are believed will uncover evidence of a crime or a person's involvement in it.

Prohibition—the nationwide ban on the manufacture, sale, and importation of alcoholic beverages under the Eighteenth Amendment. The term also refers to the period during which this amendment was in effect.

prohibitionist—an advocate of Prohibition.

ratification—an official approval of a legal document such as a constitution.

referendum (plural: *referenda*)—a referral to the voters of a political question such as a law, a new constitution, or an amendment to an existing constitution.

sovereign—a person or organization not under the control of another.

sovereign immunity—a doctrine that forbids individuals from filing lawsuits against a government without its consent.

sovereignty—the power to govern.

suffrage—the right to vote for the election of public officials.

suffragist—a supporter of voting rights for women.

temperance—using alcoholic beverages in moderation or abstaining from their use. Some advocates of temperance also support restricting or prohibiting the sale of such beverages.

trial—a formal examination in a court of law to determine a particular issue, such as whether a person has committed a crime.

warrant—an official order authorizing a public official to perform a particular act.

BIBLIOGRAPHY

Anastaplo, George. *The Amendments to the Constitution*. Baltimore: Johns Hopkins University Press, 1995.

Faber, Doris and Harold. *We the People: The Story of the United States Constitution Since 1787*. New York: Charles Scribner's Sons, 1987.

Feeley, Malcolm M., and Samuel Krislow. *Constitutional Law*. Boston: Little, Brown & Co., 1985.

Flexner, Eleanor. *Century of Struggle*. New York: Atheneum, 1974.

Foner, Eric. *Reconstruction, 1863-1877: America's Unfinished Revolution*. New York: Harper & Row, 1988.

Franklin, John Hope. *Reconstruction After the Civil War*. 2d ed. Chicago: The University of Chicago Press, 1994.

Fuller, Raymond. *Child Labor and the Constitution*. New York: Thomas Y. Crowell Co., 1923.

Garraty, John A., ed. *Quarrels That Have Shaped the Constitution*. New York: Harper & Row, 1964.

Griffith, Elisabeth. *In Her Own Right: The Life of Elizabeth Cady Stanton*. New York: Oxford University Press, 1984.

Ireland, Tom. *Child Labor*. New York: G. P. Putnam's Sons, 1937.

Jacobs, Clyde E. *The Eleventh Amendment and Sovereign Immunity*. Westport, CT: Greenwood Press, Inc., 1972.

Kelly, Alfred H., Winfred A. Harbison, and Herman Belz. *The American Constitution: Its Origins and Development*. 6th ed. New York: W. W. Norton & Co., Inc., 1983.

Kyvig, David E. *Explicit and Authentic Acts: Amending the U.S. Constitution 1776-1995*. Lawrence: University Press of Kansas, 1996.

Leuchtenberg, William E. *Franklin D. Roosevelt and the New Deal, 1932-1940*. New York: Harper Torchbooks, 1963.

Lieberman, Jethro K. *The Evolving Constitution*. New York: Random House, 1992.

Lindop, Edmund. *Birth of the Constitution*. Hillside, NJ: Enslow Publishers, Inc., 1987.

Mathis, Doyle. "Chisholm v. Georgia: Background and Settlement." *Journal of American History*, vol. 54 (June 1967), pp. 19-29.

Mitchell, Broadus and Louis P. *A Biography of the Constitution of the United States: Its Origin, Formation, Adoption, Interpretation*. 2d ed. New York: Oxford University Press, 1975.

Nelson, William E. *The Fourteenth Amendment*. Cambridge, MA: Harvard University Press, 1988.

Orth, John V. *The Judicial Power of the United States: The Eleventh Amendment in American History*. New York: Oxford University Press, 1987.

Pole, J. R., ed. *The American Constitution For and Against: The Federalist and Anti-Federalist Papers*. New York: Hill & Wang, 1987.

Rakove, Jack. *Original Meanings: Politics and Ideas in the Making of the Constitution*. New York: Alfred A. Knopf, 1996.

Rosenberg, Rosalind. *Divided Lives: American Women in the Twentieth Century*. New York: Hill & Wang, 1992.

Schwartz, Bernard A. *A History of the Supreme Court*. New York: Oxford University Press, 1993.

Smith, Page. *The Constitution: A Documentary and Narrative History*. New York: Morrow Quill Paperbacks, 1980.

Sunstein, Cass R. *The Partial Constitution*. Cambridge, MA: Harvard University Press, 1993.

Vose, Clement E. *Constitutional Change: A Twentieth Century Fund Study*. Lexington, MA: Lexington Books, 1972.

Warren, Charles. *The Supreme Court in United States History*. Vol. I. Boston: Little, Brown & Co., 1922.

INDEX

Page numbers in *italics* refer to illustrations.

(171)

(172)